ARNA

·

The Journal of
The University of Sydney Arts Students Society

2009

ARNA 2009 first published by Darlington Press

Darlington Press is an imprint of SYDNEY UNIVERSITY PRESS

Funded by the University of Sydney Union and the University of Sydney Faculty of Arts.

Editors: Nancy Lee
        Callie Henderson

Images and some short quotations have been used in this book. Every effort has been made to identify and attribute credit appropriately. The editors thank contributors for permission to reproduce their work.

Fisher Library F03, University of Sydney, NSW 2006 Australia
Email: info@sup.usyd.edu.au

ISBN 978-1-921364-10-5

Design and layout by Khym Scott

for all young writers

Credits

Contents

Foreword

A year after its 2008 resurrection from the archives, *ARNA* is back to stimulate and literate. From the start I've wanted this journal to shine like the bright minds enclosed in its pages. We received so many submissions, and the variety of topics and genres is something we have strived to reflect in this publication.

I wanted *ARNA* to be a showcase of the talent that fills the Arts faculty and the wider University community. Printed here are analytical essays of depth and insight, creative stories of humour and intelligence, poetry of loss and of love, social commentary and reflective satire.

I've always felt that history is in the hands of those who take the time to chronicle it. That is just one of the reasons I think it is so important for writers to be encouraged and invited to contribute to our little world of lectures and Great Halls. The University would be truly bereft without the diverse and inquiring minds that penned these snippets of literary soup.

When I took a blind leap into the SASS Publications pool, I was unsure of what I was really getting myself into. Almost a year later I am so glad of my impetuousness. Journals are tricky things to organise. There is so much to account for, so much to consider, so many stumbling points. Editing *ARNA* has been such a fantastic challenge.

Thank you to the sub editors, to the launch committee, to the numerous talented writers exploding out of the Faculty of Arts, to my mixed-bag family and of course to the best co-editor in living existence, Nancy. You made *ARNA* possible.

Enjoy this voyage into Artsy penmanship, and remember: if you see a boundary, eat it, and wash it down with a cup of hot steaming rules.

Callie Henderson

loud house

Rosa Valerie Campbell

In the big yellow house we drank coffee every morning.

After we ran out of mugs, we would drink from jars that caught the bright Sydney morning sun. Curled up, warm from sleep, squatting on the deck, staring at our toes,

all six of us willing ourselves awake.

Besides the early quiet, our bodies creaking awake as the house expanded with the sun,

there was always talking. We would take our jar cups into the bathroom as others ran baths or peed,

not willing to allow nudity to end the conversation.

We would press each other for more, catch one another's breath, run alongside and then, inevitably, smash into each other's sentences.

For two years my days were punctuated with someone crashing through my door announcing, "Sorry, I just had an urgent thought!"

We always said sorry and we never were.

When the yellow house became black in the night, we would pull up chairs, throw down plates and eat together.

I never heard the scrape of a fork against a plate, against a knife the whole time I was there.

I know everything about these women;

the intricacies of their voices,

the way their particular pain travels on their tongues,

the way their lips smile,

the shapes of their tears,

their kind of quivering.

But I do not know how they sound when they chew.

casual friday

Courtney Tight

jimmy pulls on his stone-washed jeans,
matches it with a red and yellow sweater-vest,
a blue shirt and some hi-top sneakers,
heads off to work.

it's casual friday! (yay!)

the day when pamela wears her "marathon 96"
tee with glee (and a polka dot skirt),
when martin puts on his spinning yo-yo belt,
when nicola, the boss, has flats instead of heels.

water cooler conversation turns to the weekend,
and its plans of golf, picnics, times with the missus –
much better than talk of the latest project
or sales pitch or the boardroom.

according to recent surveys,
casual fridays boost employee happiness,
increases lunch room cake intake
and copy room fucking.

it's casual friday! (yay!)

when jimmy goes home
to his lovely wife,
she asks him, "how was your day?"
and if it's a casual friday,
jimmy smiles and says, "pretty good,
i got to wear my sweater-vest!"

Consuming 'Man Candy':
Teen Idols and the Feminine Adolescent Gaze

Bridie Connellan

Teenhood is an era shuffling awkwardly between the binaries of innocence and experience, when young females find themselves exposed to the realms of an intriguing, often intimidating and indecipherable species: boys. But with pin-up princes from Hollywood lining bedroom walls and a host of media portraying such figures in a strikingly flattering light, the possibility of watching a fantasy dream boy can become significantly more appealing than realistic encounters with pubescent testosterone. This essay will explore how the construction of the male teen idol is both an effective means for female adolescents to gauge introductions to the opposite sex in a non-threatening manner, as well as providing an avenue through which they may project their own desires and fantasies of what such a male should be while growing up. This essay will discuss how marketing is crucial to the construction of the female adolescent spectator, and how capitalising on teen girl hysteria since the 1960s is a readily seized opportunity for various media outlets with a boy to sell.

The image of the contemporary screaming teenage girl overcome with adoration for a particular male pin-up is not without generational precedent, with 1960s Beatlemania analysed by Ehrenreich, Hess and Jacobs as "an epidemic"[1] of teenage fanaticism. Almost 50 years later, the female psyche has changed little as teen idols or 'heartthrobs' of popular culture continue to send swoons through flocks of giggling, screaming devotees queued for a fleeting glimpse of the boys who have bedecked their walls for the past six months. In her psychoanalysis of 'Visual Pleasure and Narrative

---

[1] Ehrenreich, Hess, & Jacobs, 1992, p.97.

Cinema', Laura Mulvey discusses Sigmund Freud's analysis of 'scopophilia' and the pleasure of looking with fascination at the human form as "taking other people as objects, subjecting them to a controlling and curious gaze".[2] For teenage girls, the exhibitionist construction of film, television and magazines starring a particularly attractive male form not only allows an unthreatening chance to gaze upon the opposite sex, but permits a projection of fantasy onto a subject who is displayed specifically for such pleasure. Of particular note to be discussed presently is Stephenie Meyer's 2005 highly successful vampiric romance novel series *Twilight*, which has generated an overwhelming response since its 2008 film release. Through lingering close-up shots, narrative perspective and clever external marketing, British actor Robert Pattinson's portrayal of the male protagonist Edward Cullen takes on the essence of what Mulvey says connotes "to-be-looked-at-ness"[3] in a way that has subverted the traditional notions of feminine objectification and masculinity. As musical comedy group 'Dolls Cabaret' sung at the 2009 Melbourne Comedy Festival, "Every teenage girl should have an Edward".[4]

However despite the angst-ridden nature of the *Twilight* narrative, teen texts are an effective means to explore such a subversion of female objectification particularly in the sense of satire and parody that appeals to a teen sense of humour and affords girls the chance to laugh at themselves. Mark Waters' 2004 film *Mean Girls* capitalises on the humour derived from the frivolity of female spectatorship and the triviality of girls watching boys, as he introduces the object of affection for the main teen female protagonist Cady Heron (Lindsay Lohan). The entrance of typically desirable character Aaron Samuels (Jonathon Bennett) is accompanied by classic string music

---

[2] Mulvey, 1975, p.8.

[3] *Ibid.*

[4] Miller, 2009.

reminiscent of 1930s romance as the object of Cady's gaze turns in slow motion in order for both the character and the audience to take in his features. While the scene intends to be humorous and clichéd in its depiction of the dream boy, with Cady's jaw dropping slightly and Aaron himself giving a wry smile, it nevertheless seeks to set up a common activity of the teenage girl: boy-watching. While certainly not a celebrity frenzy in the wider sense, this encounter parodies teen spectatorship, and it is of interest to note that actor Jonathon Bennett was a featured 'Crush to Watch' on the *Dolly* magazine website for several weeks after *Mean Girls'* release.[5]

Such an example is merely fiction, but as Engle and Kesser's study argues, celebrity idolization is thus "an avenue through which girls explore romantic views and attitudes toward interpersonal relationships"[6] and therefore never actually require physical contact with the object of their gaze. Construction of 'Who's Hotter'[7] online polls by *Dolly* magazine or *Girlfriend* magazine photo spreads aptly named 'Man Candy'[8] serve explicitly to line up the male objects as items for viewing, judging and consuming, allowing young females the chance to survey the 'variety' of males out there without having to embark on physical decisions of sexual experience or relationships. As John Berger argued in his 'Ways of Seeing', "Images were first made to conjure up the appearance of something that was absent".[9]

---

[5] Jonathon Bennett: Crush to Watch (2004).

[6] Engle & Kasser, 2005, p.264.

[7] 'Who's Hotter' Online Poll (2009).

[8] 'Man Candy: Robert Pattinson', *Girlfriend*, January 2009, p.45.

[9] Berger, 1972, p.109.

Such a distance between looking at and touching a desired object that is not quite ready to be experienced is of particular interest when such celebrity objects are significantly older than their admirers. For example, *Twilight*'s Robert Pattinson, despite portraying 'high school student' Edward Cullen, is 23 years old, a decidedly large age gap from his teen aficionados who have yet to cover such developmental ground. Vladimir Nabokov's controversial 1959 novel *Lolita* toys with this notion of projecting immature fantasies on an older male, with the young female protagonist Dolores Haze attaching cinematic notions of romance to the apparently handsome middle-aged stranger who comes to reside in her house. Chapter 16 describes a scene in which this stranger, Humbert Humbert, discovers a poster of a striking movie star, who supposedly bears resemblance to himself, attached to the 12-year-old's bedroom wall and notices, "Lo had drawn a jocose arrow to the haggard lover's face and had put, in block letters: H.H".[10] This scene depicts an instance in which the consistent Freudian scopophilia of the elder male predator is subverted, and the gaze of the feminine adolescent is exposed for its voyeuristic and somewhat juvenile tendencies. However the horror of Lolita lies in the male object's audacity to act on what he perceives to be a besotted attraction on behalf of his step-daughter, crossing the threshold of Mulvey's detached gaze in which "only sexual satisfaction can come from watching".[11]

Nevertheless, Stuart Hall and Paddy Whannel argue that the pop stars teenage girls admire "are not remote stars, but tangible idealisations of the life of the average teenager"[12] and are thus considered by both the girls themselves and their parental supervisors as non-threatening and relatable objects of admiration. Characters such as Robert Pattinson's Edward

---

[10] Nabokov, 1959, Chapter 16.

[11] Mulvey, 1975, p.9.

[12] Hall, & Whannel, 1965, p.35.

Cullen (*Twilight*), Zac Efron's Troy Bolton (*High School Musical*) or teen film-band sensation The Jonas Brothers (*Camp Rock*) are distinctly boyish and almost prepubescently feminine in their appearance, rarely seen to be sporting facial hair or anything considered ruggedly or roughly masculine. Regardless of Pattinson's vampiric character in the film version of Meyer's novel, these 'dream boys' are never portrayed as predators or anything more than good abstinent boys who stand on the innocent cusp of adulthood. As Catherine Driscoll argues, "these pop stars are often assumed to be boys rather than men"[13] and as such they are neither physically or sexually threatening to their female admirers. Teen texts such as *Twilight* and *High School Musical* depict the male protagonists denying their teen female counterparts' sexual advances and opting for abstinence, with Edward Cullen aptly remarking in Meyer's *Twilight* successor *Eclipse*, "Bella ... would you please stop trying to take your clothes off?"[14] Placing these decidedly anti-macho characters in a position of defense allows teenage girls to feel empowered in their gaze upon fantasy. With a reflection on the 1960s that still resonates with young females today, Ehrenreich, Hess and Jacobs argue that "Very young 'women' are still a little frightened of the idea of sex. Therefore they feel safer worshipping idols who don't seem too masculine, or too much the 'he man' ".[15] Thus the juvenile, clean-shaven Zac Efron is awarded yet another *Dolly* magazine photo spread while rugged, manly and sexually potent Hugh Jackman is confined to the more mature pages of *Marie Claire*.

Essentially, these teen male figures of spectatorship are never actually meant to be touched and thus remain 'safe' objects for young girls to gaze upon. Girls may read up on

---

[13] Driscoll, 2002, p.270.

[14] Meyer, 2007, p.450.

[15] Ehrenreich, Hess, & Jacobs, 1992, p.102.

their 'dream boy' and his likes, dislikes and favourite food in order to engage in what Laurence Grossberg discusses as "the sensibility of fandom",[16] however ultimately the figure pictured on their bedroom wall is nothing more than an image to gaze upon. As Engle and Kasser argue, "Fans frequently treat male celebrities as mere sex objects, not as individuals with personalities and their own subjective experience",[17] and thus visual texts in popular culture from film to television to magazine covers, are deliberately constructed for what Mulvey describes as "skilled and satisfying manipulation of visual pleasure".[18] The teen girl's pleasure often lies in the ability to look and not touch as a sexually immature age bracket beginning to be exposed to the libidinous tendencies of hormonally charged pubescent boys. Bella Swan, *Twilight*'s pensive female protagonist even initially allows herself such a safe position of spectatorship and intrigued pleasure as she ponders,

> If I was being honest with myself, I knew I was eager to get to school because I would *see* Edward Cullen. And that was very, very stupid.[19] (Emphasis added.)

However, despite such an in-text communication of teen attraction, the voyeurism surrounding the character of Edward Cullen and his filmic portrayer Robert Pattinson has even seeped outside the text itself and publicised a culture of 'girls watching boys' that finds recent precedent in the boy band hysteria of the 1990s. Using such a narrative device of voyeurism, with Bella described by critics as "the

---

[16] Grossberg, 1992, p.50.

[17] Engle, & Kasser, 2005, p.268.

[18] Mulvey, 1975, p.8.

[19] Meyer, 2005, p.54.

aggressive pursuer",[20] it is not surprising that majority of *Twilight* readers or "Twihards"[21] jostle for a film peek at what Meyer constructs as "this beautiful boy".[22] Columnist for *The Guardian*, Bidisha, nicely summarises the filmic Bella's voyeuristic position as a teen female gazer as she comments, "For the whole film, [Edward] is the object, she the boyish beholder, the desirer, the wanter, the one who says, 'You're beautiful'. And upon seeing him for the first time, the entire cinema gave a groan of longing".[23] In a developmental period of confusion and sexual maturity, such a narrative has been critiqued as quite revolutionary in terms of subverting male scopophilia, particularly in that young female sexual fantasy remains, at least for the first novel, unthreatening fantasy. It is this fantasy however, that makes for exceptionally successful marketing.

As Engle and Kesser argue, "it must not be ignored that celebrities often come prepackaged, ready to be marketed to the public".[24] Despite the success of Meyer's novel, engagement with the narrative often seems to stem outside the text, particularly with its film release, with celebrity culture packaged under the *Twilight* brand for easy consumption in what Catherine Driscoll discusses as "the girl market".[25] With merchandise, fansites and posters enlarging the actors portraying Edward Cullen and his competitive character Jacob Black to an almost life-size proportion, the narrative of voyeurism and romantic attachment steps outside the pages of the novel and into the bedrooms of a sizeable teen

---

[20] Voynar. 2008.

[21] 'About: Vampire Twilight', 2008.

[22] Meyer, 2005, p.50.

[23] Bidisha, 2009.

[24] Engle, & Kasser, 2005, p.268.

[25] Driscoll, 2002, p.267.

demographic. Thus, the redefined feminine gaze does not simply exist in itself amidst the realm of the teenage girl but is actively marketed to such susceptible consumers.

Teenage girls are often targeted for their high consumption of popular culture as a means for socialisation and development of identities and tastes. As Driscoll argues, "An idea of the girl market is employed to sell participation in girlhood".[26] Distinctive personalities become fashionable to admire, with marketing tools such as the now-online *Missbehave* magazine's concept of 'Crush Alerts'[27] setting the standard of which male idols are in vogue for engaging in the current trends of popular culture and being a quintessential 'girl'. *Twilight* in particular has become a tool of marketing hype in selling the male characters to a young female audience, with teen magazine *Cosmo Girl* heavily advertising their *'Twilight Boys Photo Shoot'*,[28] while the *New York Post*'s online popular culture blog *PopWrap* constantly advertises forums and poll-related articles entitled *'Twilight* Boys: Who's Hotter Now?'[29] Assigning the male subjects nicknames in so-called "teenspeak",[30] for example Robert Pattinson's abbreviated moniker 'RPATTZ', or the Jonas Brothers' collective 'JoBro', further establishes their material purpose as products for teen consumption and reinvigorates the novelty of inspection. Such adoring frenzy is crucial to the commercial success of such idols and enhance the sexual yearnings from admirers, as Ehrenreich, Hess and Jacobs reflect on the Jonas Brothers' 60s predecessors, "Hysteria was critical to the marketing of

---

[26] Driscoll, 2002, p.267.

[27] Arfin, 2009.

[28] Katz, 2008.

[29] Wieselman, 2009.

[30] Meyer, 1994.

the Beatles."[31] Far from being the objectified bearers of the masculine gaze, teen girls have the benefit of being prime consumers to be supplied with ample viewing material. Thus, the basic notion of 'who's watching who' in the youth market becomes essentially a question of supply and demand.

By subverting the traditionally masculine spectatorship emblematic in the majority of popular culture texts, the female adolescent's sexually developmental stage allows such objectification to place male subjects under a new and curious gaze, where judgement and harmless voyeurism allow curiosity to remain fantasy. While this often consumerist demographic finds itself exposed to commercial culture and blatant marketing in regards to these 'heartthrobs', the construction of boy-like teen idols provides a means for which girls can garner pleasure simply from looking as the hormonal and sexual aspects of their identity take shape. While certainly real life experience and socialisation processes are intrinsic to feminine youth development in this period of confusion and self-discovery, ultimately, two-dimensional boys won't break their hearts.

[31] Ehrenreich, Hess, & Jacobs, 1992, p.99.

Bibliography

'About: Vampire *Twilight*', (2008). Vampire *Twilight* [Online Blog]. Available at http://www.vampiretwilight.com/about/. Retrieved 2 April 2009.

Arfin, L. (2009). 'New Crush Alert!' *Missbehave Magazine* [Online], 22 April 2009. Available at http://www. missbehavemag.com/new-crush-alert/. Retrieved 23 April, 2009.

Berger, J. (1972). *Ways of Seeing*. Hammondsworth: Penguin.

Bidisha. (2009). 'Bitten by the Female Gaze', *The Guardian* [Online]. 19 January 2009. Available at http://www. guardian.co.uk/commentisfree/2009/jan/19/women-gender. Retrieved 3 April 2009.

Bradshaw, P. (2008). 'Film Review: *Twilight*', *The Guardian* [Online] 19 December 2008. Available at http://www. guardian.co.uk/film/2008/dec/19/film-review-twilight-teen-vampire. Retrieved 3 April 2009.

Bulloch, B. (2009). 'At the Admiral: *Twilight* Makes Abstinence Sexy', *West Seattle Herald* [Online] 20 February 2009. Available at http://www.westseattleherald. com/2009/02/19/features/admiral-twilight-makes-abstinence-sexy. Retrieved 5 April 2009.

Driscoll, C. (2002). 'The Girl Market and Girl Culture', in *Girls*, (pp.264–344). New York: Columbia University Press.

Durham, M.G. (1998). 'Dilemmas of desire: The representation of adolescent sexuality in two teen magazines.' *Youth and Society*, 29(3):369.

Ehrenreich, B., Hess, E. and Jacobs, G. (1992). 'Beatlemania: Girls Just Want to Have Fun', in Lewis, L.A. (Ed), *The Adoring Audience*, (pp.84–106). New York: Routledge.

Engle, Y. & Kasser, T. (2005). 'Why Do Adolescent Girls Idolize Male Celebrities?', *Journal of Adolescent Research*, 20(2):263–283.

Goldman, E. (2004). '"Knowing" Lolita: Sexual Deviance and Normality in Nabokov's Lolita', *Nabokov Studies*, 8:87–104.

Grossberg, L. (1992). 'Is There a Fan in the House? The Affective Sensibility of Fandom', in Lewis, L.A. (Ed), *The Adoring Audience*, (pp.50–65). New York: Routledge.

Hall, S. & Whannel, P. (1965). *The Popular Arts*. New York: Pantheon Books.

Jacobsson, E.M. (1999). *A Female Gaze?* Stockholm: Royal Institute of Technology.

Katz, N. (2008). '*Twilight* Boys "Cosmo Girl" Photo Shoot', *Junior Celebs* [Online]. 18 November 2008. Available at http://www.juniorcelebs.com/twilight-boys-cosmo-girl-photo-shoot/. Retrieved 2 April 2009.

Mean Girls (2004). Dir. Mark S. Waters, Paramount: United States of America, 97 mins.

Meyer, L. (1994). *Teenspeak: A Bewildered Parent's Guide to Teenagers*, Princeton: Peterson's.

Meyer, S. (2005). *Twilight*. New York: Little, Brown and Company.

Meyer, S. (2006). *New Moon*. New York: Little, Brown and Company.

Meyer, S. (2007). *Eclipse*. New York: Little, Brown and Company.

Meyer, S. (2008). *Breaking Dawn*. New York: Little, Brown and Company.

Mulvey, L. (1975). 'Visual Pleasure and Narrative Cinema', *Screen*, 16(3):6–18.

Nabokov, V. (1959). *Lolita*, UK: Penguin Modern Classics, Penguin.

Nash, I (2002). '"Nowhere Else to Go": *Gidget* and the Construction of Adolescent Femininity', *Feminist Media Studies*, 2:3.

Sweeney, G. (1994). 'The Face on the Lunch Box: Television's Construction of the Teen Idol', *Velvet Light Trap*, No. 33, Austin: University of Texas Press.

Turan, K. (2008). '*Twilight*: For Teens, A Swooningly Risky Romance', *NPR* [Online], Movie Reviews, 21 November 2008. Available at http://www.npr.org/templates/story/story.php?storyId=97210195. Retrieved 5 April 2009.

Twilight (2008). Dir. Catherine Hardwicke, Summit Entertainment: United States of America, 122 mins.

Voynar, K. (2008). '*Twilight*: Sometimes a Sexual Fantasy is Just a Sexual Fantasy', Movie City News: *Voynaristic* [Online]. 24 November 2008. Available at http://www.moviecitynews.com/columnists/voynar/2008/081124.html. Retrieved 3 April 2009.

Wald, G. (2002). "'I Want It That Way": Teenybopper Music and the Girling of Boy Bands', *Genders OnLine Journal*, 35, Available at http://www.genders.org/g35/g35_wald.html. Retrieved 20 May 2009.

'Who's Hotter' Online Poll, (2009). Dollywood, *Dolly* [Online]. Available at http://dolly.ninemsn.com.au/whoshotter/ Retrieved 2 April 2009.

Wieselman, J. (2009). '*Twilight* Boys: Who's Hotter Now?', *New York Post*: PopWrap [Online]. 27 February 2009. Available at http://blogs.nypost.com/popwrap/ archives/2009/02/twilight_hotter.html. Retrieved 2 April 2009.

Heil Hitler!

Michael Barnes

Joe Stalin, by all accounts,
Is history's greatest killer;
Thirty million or more, they say,
Far deadlier than Attila.
Singly, and in job lots,
He'd shunt them to Siberia;
In terror ranks he had no cause
To think himself inferior.
This gross deception did not end
With Joe in pose, avuncular,

Complete with mo, Saddam Hussein
Was at heart, carbuncular.
What is it with these dictators,
These tyrants of modernity,
With souls depraved which hide behind
Bland features of fraternity?

Papa Doc of Haiti fame
Essayed a bedside manner,
Yet terrorised his humble folk
With fear and hate and hammer;
While other despots dealt in death
Without any fancy to-do,
Papa and his Ton-Ton thugs
Called in Satan and voodoo.

Now take Pol Pot, his killing fields,
Whose smiling radiant face
Disguised his liquidation of
A quarter of his race

And let's not forget the Africans
With their Megawatti smiles;
Mugabe, killer through and through,
In spite of his denials;
Idi Amin, the chief buffoon,
Who thought it rather fun
To crack a joke as he slaughtered 'em,
In groups, or one by one.

When you work it through, the only one
To break this ghoulish mould
Was Führer of the German Reich,
Crazed father of his fold.
He'd rant and rave and bump 'em off
His eyes insanely lit,
Most murderous of the bloody lot,
But not a hypocrite.

Man as Art: On Seeing Monet and the Impressionists

Sam Lewin

People think that God is a sculptor, that from clay he fashioned Adam, drawing up with it no small amount of mud to create man. And when people think this they say to themselves: "Ah! But what else?" You cannot have such a relationship with words, with pictures. One cannot truly feel oneself mirrored, have such affinity with something one cannot walk around, and which portrays such perfect beauty. You feel that the stone breathes, that the stone yearns to move, to embrace you even. There is no canvas upon which it is painted; there are no notes that must be read, no instrument; there is no code on paper, which expresses some distorted ideal. There is but this grand figure, this being, whose simultaneity expresses motion, who is self-contained, needing no other medium for its portrayal but existing as a portrayal of itself. In seeing this perfection you think that sculpture is the most divine art, that God is clearly a sculptor, that this form alone betrays His secret visions of beauty. There are no shadows in sculpture. One is tempted to say that it is the only art. You are tempted to say that whatever is, is good.

But God is not a sculptor. We stand as proof that he does not have the patience. He was an Impressionist the day He painted Adam, a surgeon when He created Eve; and He remains these things. When you first see His paintings, you are overwhelmed with sensation. Unlike anything before them, and certainly unlike any sculpted form, you are convinced of motion, of a swiftness and light. It is not light as one would see a flash, or the flicker of a flame, nor is it the static light of day. It is filtered and tempered, revealed in the strokes of the brush as something of infinite speed, so fast as to be motionless, but revealed as embodied softness in a frozen moment, as it caresses the luscious grass, the leaves *Or pur*, as it pushes through the water's vapours to cast in blue the façade of a cathedral, or paint in warmth some pastoral scene, to both conceal and therein illuminate the shadows. It rustles leaves like wind. It is light that moves so fast in timelessness as to make all other forms ice. No shadow can exist without this light, which casts its blessings indiscriminately, which makes everything His, everything holy. Tears form in the corner of your eye, and you feel embarrassed, but these crystal drops that cloud your sight simply refract the vision, a dazzling concoction of that reflected light, so that you float in light, and you feel for sure that whatever is, is right.

Like a desperate blind man or a leper you rush forward, prostrating yourself at His feet. You dare not look up, perhaps out of fear, but you do not know of what. The artist loves praise, appreciation, needs it even; and you, as a work of such vitality, equal in beauty, have every right to stand shoulder to shoulder with this masterwork, to be displayed even, as an avatar of beauty, an incarnation of God, as indeed art is an avatar of the artist's sense of beauty. But when you look up you see nothing. There are confused swirls, frenzied strokes that cut across the canvas, that cut through you to the bone and make it weep. The tones are wrong; the brown is purple; the orange that looked so vital is a forlorn beige; the water's pale blue has been robbed of its fire and is but a pastel wall over surging and misplaced bottle and apple greens and falling flecks of white. The texture of the paint itself is as careless as the light, which you see will illuminate everything, both the beautiful and the ugly. Your flaws are laid bare for all to see; when you are inspected you are pulled apart limb by limb and none will notice the pleasing taste of your hair, or the scents of fruit that perfume your neck. One sees the rotting layer of skin, an oil stain on your dress, which is made worse by the dress' very quality. It comes as a shock to see this, so suddenly, to realise that you were so absorbed in the light as to miss completely the form upon which it fell.

You cannot help but question your faith in His creation. He has bestowed upon you the gift of sight, cleared your misty eyes and cured you. But He has given you nothing to look at. What reasons could He have for this, you ask yourself. Is it a test of your faith in Him; perhaps we are to find beauty and not have it given to us. Is it that He is but one of us? It could be that He is incapable of creating beauty in life, as we are, and granted us only His own sense of beauty that we might see it in art. That seems very likely. Why should the artist care for His canvas even half as much as for his painting, except that it is needed for support? Perhaps He does not exist at all. For it is inevitable that one comes to believe this: that whatever is, is wanting. So you rush back, hurriedly, with eyes squeezed tightly shut and with an anxious pattering in your chest, as though a child were skipping on your heart. You realise that you should look not at the paint but at the picture. At once all your passion and powerful feelings come rushing back. But you cannot forget that man Himself is but an impression, and you will never be satisfied with Him.

untitled i

Audrey Menezes

you spoke to me on crisp white linens
    & ran to bed wanting to fly out
    windows

        and you called me your moon and said
      mountains were nothing
        choices were mine and
        we could swing like broken
            pendulums every night
        if we wanted

with forgotten keys to my forgotten locks in my back pocket
    I want to open you up so I can stitch you closed
      but your points are too blunt, my love, and
    sticks too thick
      believe me, believe me (and you don't)

so what to do when my ears don't catch your smile
    and lilies brown from inside out

I'm all grown up
    but let me feel your nose against my cheek
  while infomercials play in the background
      talking into your shoulder and tasting coke & Twix

      and let the world wonder
        why waste our whispers

Silence is Golden?

Gillian Brooks

Many sources of ancient wisdom, from the Book of Proverbs in the Bible to the maxims of Pubilius Syrus, maintain that a fool can hide ignorance through silence: saying nothing is much wiser than saying something for the sake of hearing the sound of one's voice. In modern times, however, the attitude has reversed: when we hear nothing, we assume ignorance. This would have something to do with the decline of a social regard for wisdom in the modern world. We much prefer mantras and catchphrases, often sprouted on bumper stickers and gift-shop key chains. But it has become a simple truth that the Quiet Person no longer holds a position of power in society – a position that finds itself in need of defence.

Can you gain or achieve anything by being quiet? It seems, rather, that there is something inherently wrong with the Quiet Person. They get overwhelmed by the barrage of words, flounder in the strong currents of opinion of which others seem to navigate so skilfully. Silence comes easily. The opposite – whatever that may be: expression? Conversation? Commotion? Noise? – is far more challenging, at least for the Quiet Person. This poses the question of which state, silence or speaking, is the default of our human nature. Our ability to communicate through speech and language is something that marks us uniquely among animals – but communication is governed by rules and relevance. We speak because it's necessary; when we have a need, or when something changes. One would assume that silence has similar motivations working behind it. Or silence could be seen to come about due to a lack of need or change. In this way, silence comes to seem lacking, failed, and flawed. So too, do those who practise silence: the Quiet People.

Silence: the dictionary defines it as the absence of noise or speech. Something lacking. But 'quiet' – that seems to have some virtue. It is also lacking, but it lacks those things that are negative, those things that clutter our minds and emotions, that create impenetrable walls of opinion. Now, in contrast, consider *Quiet*: with little noise; calm or tranquil; untroubled. There's something soothing and sustaining about quiet: it suggests we need it to balance out the clutter of noise and talk. They coexist, mutually exclusive yet symbiotic, like yin and yang. Like light and shade, like sweet and sour, like day and night, one cannot exist without the other.

On what level do we achieve this balance? Looking broadly, perhaps we aim for two complementary societal groups: the Quiet People and the Eloquent Ones. But to separate silence and speech at this scale creates conflict, each group being offended and annoyed by something as seemingly innocuous as the other's use of words.

In this way, the (a new word is needed here – Articulate? Vocal? Eloquent? Verbose? Loud?) Ones might claim that silence creates, or at least perpetuates, a lot of problems: apathy, indifference, impressions of stupidity, ignorance, ineptitude, rudeness. Above all, if someone makes no contribution to a debate, their position is ambiguous, appearing uncertain or possibly insecure. However, so much talk in the world is born of insecurity: it occurs just because it is expected. A contribution, for the sake of avoiding insecurity, is just as questionable as that of the Quiet Person.

The social artifice of coherence is a well-rehearsed script, most certainly. Is it really such a terrible thing to simply not know, or to fail in finding no way to express a reaction or emotion other than silence? Think of how we respond, deep within ourselves, to things like death and suffering. Silence.

Dumb-struckness. The rawest form of communication, silence can have its own particular eloquence and fluency.

The pressure of everyday life has forced me to strive for sharper articulation. Why don't I speak? Because I am content. No – because I am afraid of the potential failure loaded in the words I plan to use. No – because I am shy. The reason that substantiates it for me is this: because I am, by nature, quiet. Can it really be as simple as that? If so, this whole article has been a contradiction: not knowing anything for certain, I have stumbled around with a few thoughts and phrases, creating an opinion for opinion's sake when, really, it might have been much more beneficial to simply remain quiet – in all senses of the word, not only silent but also calm, tranquil and untroubled – and let someone else, or something else, perhaps even silence itself, do the talking.

Picking Up the Pages:
An Analysis of the Materiality of Magazines

Joy Enriquez

An introduction to the world of microzines

> Everything at Mag Nation can be touched, felt and
> browsed except for our staff.
> [Shop sign in magazine retail store 'Mag Nation',
> Melbourne, Victoria]

Magazines, in their traditional sense, are dying. Consumer
titles that have dominated news stands for over 250 years
are now evolving in an attempt to convert the seemingly
outdated print medium into the increasingly pervasive and
popular online platform. A strong online presence benefits
publications by providing readers with supplementary
material, more detailed coverage, and a richer multimedia
experience.[1] Because of these benefits, there are real concerns
that magazines will die with the growth of online content.
Increasing media consumption via the Internet by way of RSS
feeds and dedicated websites signal the extinction of the printed
periodical similarly to the way e-book readers will eventually
see the death of the book.[2] However, what many people do
not realise is that the introduction of computer technology –
particularly that of desktop publishing tools to skilled youths
with large supplies of creative ideas, ambition, time, contacts
and caffeine – has signalled the emergence of an enduring
category of print publications. Some call these independent
magazines, small magazines, or microzines. David Renard
refers to these publications as the 'stylepress'; "physically and
aesthetically engaging, vibrant chroniclers of trends", that

---

1 Holmes, 2008, p.148.

2 Yen, 2008, p.35.

exist not just as platforms for ideas and artistic expressions, but as a showcase of a current cultural experience, produced as visual pleasures as well as enduring artefacts.[3]

Microzines are loosely defined as beautifully designed, producer-owned and made, serial print publications that have small circulation and high production values.[4] These publications are unique objects, described by Angelo Cirimele, publisher of *Magazine* as "small jewels for connoisseurs" of which the general public is unaware.[5] They have a distinct place in the print genealogy, adopting their aesthetical and counter-cultural values from their predecessor, the zine. Zines are hand-made magazines or mini-comics about anything and everything – bands, movies, subcultures, obsessions, rants, reviews, poems, photos and essays. They are distinct from commercial publications or today's blogs in that they are tactile (usually made of paper, cardboard, or fabric which is stitched, glued or stapled together), are not efficient to produce (often drawn or written by hand and photocopied), are made by individuals or small teams (as opposed to large publishing houses), and exist for small, niche audiences (as opposed to large groups of global consumers).[6] *MixTape, The Tilted Page* and *Tiny Paper Hearts* are just a few examples of over 50 Australian zine titles that visited the Museum of Contemporary Art for the 2009 Sydney Writers' Festival. These zines are sold in bookstores, clothing shops and online vendors around Australia and successfully document the art and culture of the present day, combined with the freedom and thrill that comes with independent publishing.

---

3 Renard, 2006, p.1.

4 Le Masurier, 2008.

5 Renard, 2006, p.2.

6 Todd, & Watson, 2006, p.13.

Microzines adopt the physical and cultural attributes of zines and merge them with the design and collaborative tools provided by digital media to create higher-end, polished publications. Titles such as *elodi*, and *Dumbo Feather Pass It On* exist not for commercial reason or gain, but to express a unique editorial vision or specific cultural philosophy – be it about skate, surf and street culture (*Monster Children*, Sydney), design and illustration (*Nico*, Luxembourg), or simple, random, ordinary life (*Karen*, Wiltshire). These publications embody similar personal qualities, creativity, labour, and the artistic and aesthetic characteristic of zines and merge these with the possibilities opened up by digital desktop publishing tools and affordable printing costs to create a larger and more durable print run.[7]

Microzines in a digital environment

Blogs, wikis, social networking sites, and the emergence of citizen and participatory journalism allow anyone with a certain degree of literacy and a decent Internet connection to publish their own thoughts and words. The online environment is perfect for communicating with global audiences, connecting niche communities with like-minded folk and providing a supposedly richer and more interactive platform for ideas-sharing and communication.[8] While this ability to collaborate and network with specific contacts has aided independent publishers by making it easier to create collaborative content, gain a following within hard-to-reach niche audiences, distribute publications and build a public presence, the consumption habits created by these electronic mediums hardly support that of print publications.[9]

---

7 Lowsowsky, 2009.

8 Thompson, 2005, p.235.

9 Anderrson, & Steedman, 2002.

Chris Chesher describes this new media space as one that favours space over time. Because digital media channels can be accessed globally by large audiences and are easily updatable, users now favour content that is fast and accessible over large distances over content that is durable and collectable. This trend towards needing up-to-date content is reflected in the ongoing popularity of easy-to-find 'Top' or 'Recent' stories on news websites, the encouragement of 'present' status updates (such as that on Facebook and Twitter) and the use of customised news listings.[10] These consumption habits pose a problem for print media because it is so easily dated – print publications take longer to produce and the moment it is produced the text cannot be updated.[11]

If the online environment provides an easier and more accessible gateway into do-it-yourself publishing, why then is this genre of print publication booming? Despite the trend for ACP Magazines and Reed Business Information towards expanding the digital version of their mainstream periodicals, the World Magazine Trends 2004/2005 states that there is optimism in the international magazine publishing market, and print on paper is likely to retain attraction for readers.[12] Mag Nation, a recently established niche magazine retailer, stocks over 4000 titles on its shelves in Melbourne.[13] In fact, microzines contribute $13 million to the global economy, and this figure is projected to grow to more than $500 million over the next two decades.[14]

---

10 Chesher, 2007, p.21.

11 Hampshire, 2006, p.31.

12 McKay, 2006, p.215.

13 Yen, 2008, p.34.

14 Renard, 2006, p.2.

Print media is akin to the cultural artefacts left behind by previous civilisations. This particular genre – the microzine – contains content that reflects a specific time, era and culture. The nature of this content – art, photography, fashion, urban trends, social commentary and personal drawings – reflects a collectability and social significance that contrasts the emphasis towards the 'now' and 'present' that digital media encompasses.

The materiality of microzines

> Clearly when we read books, we really read books – that is, we read the physicality or materiality of the book as well as and in relation to the text itself. Literacy, then, may be said to include not only textual competence but material competence, an ability to read the semiotics of the concrete forms that embody, shape, and condition the meanings of texts.[15]

One of the microzine's most defining characteristics is that of their physicality and their "slickness".[16] The microzine's emphasis on physicality and materiality – the size, shape of the book, the texture of the cover and the durability of the paper – plays an integral part in what makes it an outstanding medium. They are distinct from consumer titles such as *Cosmopolitan*, *Time*, or *Women's Weekly* because, unlike mainstream magazines, microzines are not mass produced, nor do they follow standard magazine formats. Values and key messages are expressed not just in the content but in physical components – from the microzine's design to the material on which it is published.

---

15 Moylan, & Stiles, 1996.

16 Jacovides, 2003, p.24.

As yet, digital media also lacks the ability to play with its physical attributes – texture, weight, binding and even the scent of the paper are all elements that make microzines unique. *Tank* magazine uses thick, cross-hatched matt cardboard and a large page size to emphasise the strength of its title and contents, *Dumbo Feather Pass It On* shies away from the glossy paper used in consumer titles and uses matt paper similar to that of a paperback to reflect the stories of the five individuals included in each issue and *The Wooden Toy* is packaged in cardboard so the reader has the experience of unpacking it: it contains a collectable art print in each issue and includes a certificate of authentication with each magazine (which prides itself on being 'handmade'). Similarly, the pages of *box* magazine are glossy, thick and made to last. It is the right size for portability and the right texture for display and collection.

Essentially, microzines cater to a tactile experience. Readers are encouraged to engage with the physical medium as well as the content within it (*Asian Punk Boy*, for example, is packaged in a wooden box which contains handmade contents which the reader must put together, while *Blank* magazine is delivered in a pizza box). In an era where much of human interaction is with machinery, the size, texture, weight, and even the source of the publication's paper stand out to make these publications unique.

As a result, the experience offered by microzines is unlike that of digital media. Digital texts are commonly produced to be consumed via machine in bite-sized chunks, or 'on the go'. Websites make the accessibility, searchability and storage of data far easier, and online magazine publishers use these functions to enhance the user's reading experience by encouraging efficiency and interactivity with multimedia. However, microzines are different in that they do not prize efficiency or accessibility. In contrast, they are created to be savoured, collected and often hold value *because* of their rarity.[17]

The collectability of microzines

> In a culture that celebrates case and immediacy, [publishers] are choosing to take part in a process that is deliberately messy, inefficient, and labour-intensive – they are choosing to take part in an art process.[18]

The very method of a microzine's creation – meticulous design choices, hours of collaboration (be it with a small design team or an online network of social contributors), and its labor intensive, time-consuming printing process – lends itself to being dangerously outdated. However, it is this very investment of time, skill and labour that make the microzine a valuable cultural artefact.[19] The personal and laborious investment involved in creating a physical object creates intimacy and affection between the creator and the reader and the arduous process of creating such a publication is, in part, what makes such texts so valuable.[20]

Technologists argue that the constraint of print publications as a time-bound medium will be its eventual cause of death; however, this may be the key to the microzine's resilience.[21] New information delivery methods and the replacement of old tools with new technologies imply that microzines are soon to be an outdated form of content delivery. However, print

---

17 Husni, 2007.

18 Piepmeier, 2008.

19 *Ibid.*

20 Glass, 1999, p.47.

21 Leslie, 2002.

publications offer a sense of place in a way websites cannot.[22] They have a specific place in a timeline and, due to their physical limitations, have a beginning, middle and end. Web pages, on the other hand, stand alone. There are millions of links to external pages and "there is no continuity, no real identity, no style, no familiar page-turning experience. No real beginning, no middle, and surely no satisfying end".[23] In a response to an article about virtual magazines, a reader of *Dissent* wrote,

> Well, there's the problem: virtual magazines have no physical virtues. Reading them, I feel dispossessed … because I value this finite object, where writers have committed themselves to these ideas and arguments, which I can read, and finish reading, and put aside (or throw away). And then I wait for the next issue. The waiting is a good thing. It gives me time to think about what I've just read.

Today's digital media may provide the benefit of spatial transcendence, but it does not mirror the permanence and longevity characteristic of traditional media forms. The physical nature of microzines allows for them to "cater to all five senses" – characteristic of an artefact of personal significance.[24] As physical objects, microzines have the ability to resurrect certain feelings, memories and experiences in a way digital technology cannot – what Stewart calls the "authentic experience". Stewart argues that we keep souvenirs in order to represent traces of past experiences. The smears on a page, the dog-eared corner, the scribbling in the margin all attribute to the microzine's standing as a cultural artefact.[25]

22 Sacks, 2006, p.22.

23 *Ibid.*

24 Husni, 2007 and Stewart, 1996.

25 Stewart, 1996, p.135.

The Future of the Microzine

Over the last 20 years, microzines have appeared in news stands with explosive force. The magazine industry is seeing growth in its independent publishing sector as creative teams find ways to utilise, experiment and express themselves within the assumed 'limitations' provided by the printed form. Some news stands are adopting these titles, lining their shelves with microzines from all over the world. These unique publications bring with them a certain sense of personality and richness. The distinct experience provided by picking up a tangible print publication is what the microzine genre represents.

Despite the exciting and viable offers that come from multimedia found online or in various media devices, microzines offer something unique that neither e-readers nor online webpage browsing can replace. They are highly regarded and sought after because of the personality they embody, the texture and materiality with which they evoke specific values and messages, and the experience felt when holding it in one's hands. Eventually they may be the only survivors of the print periodical, surviving only as a collectable anthology of cultural trends and creative practice. Whatever the case, in this digitally saturated era they will pose as reminders that information is not just downloadable, and a snapshot of history is not *just* available via a Google search or click of a mouse button. An equally rich, rewarding and sensually stimulating experience can be accessed – simply by picking up the pages.

Bibliography

Anderrson, P. & Steedman, J. (Ed). (2002). *Inside Magazines: Independent Pop Culture Magazines*. Corte Madera, Cal.: Gingko Press.

Cirimele, A. (2006). 'More on the Stylepress', In D. Renard (Ed), *The Last Magazine*. New York: Universe Publishing.

Glass, W.H. (1999). 'In Defense of the Book.' In *Harper's Magazine*.

Hampshire, N. (2006). 'The E-Paper Catalyst.', In D. Renard (Ed), *The Last Magazine*. New York: Universe Publishing.

Heller, S. (2006). 'Alternative Publishing in the Twentieth Century', In D. Renard (Ed), *The Last Magazine*. New York: Universe Publishing.

Holmes, T. (2006). 'Electronic Journalism and Electronic Publishing', In J. McKay (Ed), *The Magazines Handbook*. 2nd Edition. Oxon: Routledge.

Husni, S.A. (2007). 'Reaching the Modern Reader', In J. Rothstien (Ed), *Designing Magazines: Inside Periodical Design, Redesign and Branding*. New York: Allworth Press.

Jacovides, M. (2003). 'Love Me, Hate Me ... The New World of the Microzine', In J. Leslie (Ed), *Magculture: New Magazine Design*. London: Laurence King.

Le Masurier, M. (2008). *Microzines: Media of Enthusiasm*. Sydney: The University of Sydney.

Leslie, J. (2002). 'Foreword' In *magCulture: new magazine design*. London: Laurence King Publishing Ltd.

Letter to the Editor. (2003). 'Reaction to Virtual Magazines', *Dissent*, 50(3):112.

'Mike Koedinger, Jeremy Leslie and Andrew Losowksy on 'Independent Magazines', the 'Magazine Industry', 'Colophon' and their 'Personal Relationship to Magazines." http://blog.colophon2009.com/colophon-2009-interviews/. Retrieved 20 May 2009.

McKay, J. (2006). *The Magazines Handbook*. 2nd Edition. Oxon: Routledge.

Morelewicz, P. (2007). 'Beyond Zines', In J. Rothstien (Ed), *Designing Magazines: Inside Periodical Design, Redesign and Branding*. New York: Allworth Press.

Moylan, M. & Stiles, L. (1996). 'Introduction', In M. Moylan & L. Stiles, (Ed), *Reading Books: Essays on the Material Text and Literature in America*. Amherst: University of Massachusetts Press.

Piepmeier, A. (2008). 'Why Zines Matter: Materiality and the Creation of Embodied Community.' *American Periodicals*, 18(2).

Renard, D. (2006). *The Last Magazine*. New York: Universe Publishing.

Rothstien, J. (2007). 'Are Magazines More Interactive than the Web', In J. Rothstien (Ed), *Designing Magazines: Inside Periodical Design, Redesign and Branding*. New York: Allworth Press.

Ryan, W.E. & Conover, T.E. (2003). 'Magazine Design and Redesign', *Graphic Communications Today*. 4th Edition: Cengage Learning.

Sacks, B. (2006). 'The Business of Content', In D. Renard
(Ed), *The Last Magazine*. New York: Universe Publishing.

Thompson, J.B. (2005). *Books in the Digital Age: The
Transformation of Academic and Higher Education
Publishing in Britain and the United States*. Cambridge,
UK: Polity Press

Todd, M. & Watson, E.P. (2006). *Watcha Mean What's a Zine?
The Art of Making Zines and Mini-Comics*. Boston: Graphia.

A Momentary Reflection

Christina Bulbrook

This is the story of a young tree spirit who found her twin one day down by the banks of the river. She was skipping past and decided to stop and lean down to watch the fish. Instead she found her own face peering back at her and rejoiced because she had found her twin sister.

Together they ran down the river, the spirit over the rocks on the banks and her twin over the rocks in the river. Every time the spirit laughed, her twin laughed too. When she tripped, her twin tripped. The young spirit found it amazing that she had lived so much of her life without knowing about her twin sister. But when it came time to return home, her twin wouldn't come. She preferred to remain in the river. The spirit understood that her twin's home was with the fish, while her own was among the trees. So she left for the night and returned the next morning to find her twin waiting for her, ready to run again and twirl and laugh and skip up and down the riverbanks together.

Every day from then on the spirit visited the river and spent amusing hours playing and laughing with her twin. Sometimes they cried over sorrows together and other times they laughed until their sides hurt. One particular day, the spirit decided she would like to see what it was like to live where her twin lived, and to allow her sister the chance to spend time in her own world amongst the rocks and animals and trees. They spent the day together as usual, running up and down the river until the sun dropped low in the sky. At this point the spirit turned to see her twin, smiling radiantly up at her as always, and in a twirling frenzy of mad excitement she suggested they swap places for the night. Her twin nodded in agreement.

So the young tree spirit leapt into
the river to change places with her.
But she could not swim, no more than
her twin could walk. She felt the icy water pull
her under, and she was caught in its rapids,
along with her twin sister. And just as they had
run, laughed and twirled together over the banks
of the river, so together they succumbed to its rapids
and together they drowned.

For one had been made to live amongst the trees, and
the other to live in the water with the fish. Being a
physical reflection of one another did not equip one to
fulfill the role of the other. Each one has his or her place
in this *brave new world* and we must all exist as who
we were made to be without changing for the wishes of
another. Else we should drown, and the other as well.

*You were my world. You were my reflection, and I yours.
When I examined a mirror I saw you. And me. We were one.
But I tried to make myself like you, I strived to be you, the way
you wanted. I transformed myself.*

I became you. And then you were gone.

And so was I.

Driving, and late

Sam Moginie

Night-water has condensed on the windscreen,
and in the doubly-blurred light the road's twists and curves
are difficult to make out. Reflective markers mean
"go this way a little, go that, or here's another" and
a human brain, tired and appreciative of a little colour,
will agree, even if it doesn't understand.

There's something on the road – cardboard or a soft toy,
a cantaloupe, a rubber chicken, a real chicken, like from the freezer:
    by the time the thing has hit the chassis, made the noise,
    and the noise has got to your ears, and your ears get it,
    it could be anything:

distinct possibilities are my ex-girlfriend's dog, a pig
and a severed human head. It's not so much I've killed anything,
because whatever it was was dead, but I've hit it, not swerved.

The rear-view is no help, because, as we've already established,
the mirror only sees water condensed on glass, plus
my eyes, black bitumen and smudged white streetlight.
If I've hit my ex-girlfriend's dog, she will be pissed.

Epiphany at 40: A Memoir

Luz Hincapié

This story begins with an epiphany, which I experienced at the momentous age of 40. My mother was visiting me in Bogotá, Colombia, for one day on a stopover back to the US. She had spent the former month in her hometown visiting the few members of her family left there. It was a day well spent and, as always, I was prodding her for information about her story of migration, which I wished to write about.

Every time I am near her I do the same: I ask and ask and try to piece together this puzzle that was her life and is my family's story. The more she tells me the more I am amazed at all she endured and the more I wonder how she came to be so grateful and able to enjoy life so much, despite the continuous tragedy she experienced. But tragedy, she would say, is too harsh a word, preferring always to look at what she has and not what she lost.

On this particular occasion I was asking her to reveal the event that she had found the most difficult; the most heartbreaking. Was it the death of my brother, Norman? Was it my eldest sister's traumatic divorce? Maybe it was the incarceration of my brother Dago, her youngest son who was ten years older than me. She answered that she was most upset at Dago being locked up in jail for six years. I found this perplexing for I had thought she would definitely say it was Norman's death. In fact, our conversation that afternoon had revolved mostly around this event.

When Norman died, I was in my sophomore year at university, far removed both physically and emotionally from the drama that my family was going through. An adolescent immersed in my own world, I would lament how detached from this episode of family history I had been. I would especially regret not keeping in touch with him those last months, and even forgetting when I spoke to him last. I am only certain that I saw him on our last birthday together, three months before his death. We shared our birth date and on the 21st of December 1987, he turned 32 and I turned 20. I might not even remember this if it hadn't been recorded in photos of us cutting a cake and opening presents. He was already so thin in those pictures. Not that he had ever been stout but the illness was already showing, marking his face with that hollow look that I learned to recognise in AIDS patients at a time when no one really knew what it was and when medicine could not yet control it.

I cried as I sat watching my mother's painful narration of the events. I cry as I write them now: she made his favourite soup that morning, but he was only able to take a few mouthfuls. With my father's help she bathed his debilitated body. They dressed him with clean pyjamas and put him in bed. They took turns sitting next to him, reading to him, talking to him, and praying. He had little energy to speak by then. In the afternoon he asked for something to drink and even tried to talk. He went to sleep but woke up and my mother saw the moment when he made his last face, the grimace of death, the moment when the spirit leaves the flesh. She cried, but she was so grateful to God that his death had been quick, peaceful, in the house, and surrounded by his family.

They say a parent should not have to witness a child's death, but my mother had already experienced the death of two babies. In the 1950s, children died due to a lack of simple medicine in her rural town in Colombia. She worked so hard all her life to support the six surviving children. Because of them, she became a migrant, moving first to different cities within the country and then, when the situation became desperate, she got the outlandish idea of going to the United

States to work. No one she knew had ever been there, but she'd heard of a friend of a friend who did. She once told me that back then it sounded like she was going to the moon.

She was 40 years old when she took on this challenge. I was only six months old. She entrusted me to her sister, and the rest of my siblings to my dad who, after previously abandoning us, had eventually returned. I was the result of that reconciliation and was reminded of this every time I spilled my cruel feminist litany against my mother for having taken him back (after he had gone off with another woman). She had done it for us because she believed that her children needed a father and because, ultimately, she truly loved him.

Many times I have imagined my mother's arrival to the New York City of the early 1970s, to the city of disco in a country at war. The civil rights movement and the hippie movement were not fully behind, and sex, drugs, and rock'n'roll had become the youth anthem. I imagine her primly dressed, as was proper for a mature married mother of six, looking for the address of the contact who was supposed to help her. She spoke no English, had a basic elementary education and didn't even understand, until much later, that those people in her apartment were not just smoking cigarettes.

I grew up seeing how hard my mum and dad worked. My father worked and lived in a country club somewhere in New Jersey during the week. My mother had several jobs including work in a garment factory which was the closest she ever got to the skill she had learned and practised in Colombia. She was a renowned dressmaker in her native Apia. With it, and with a little shop selling miscellanea, she had successfully supported herself and her children for five years when abandoned by my father. She would continue to create beautiful dresses and clothes for her children and grandchildren. Whenever I wanted a new dress that I had seen in a window shop but could not afford, I would draw it and my mother would replicate it. For baptisms, first communions, sweet 15ths (according to the Colombian tradition) and even marriages we went shopping for the materials that my mother would use in her creations.

It's not until you mature that you start to understand the hard work and constant sacrifice that your parents went through for your sake. Nor do children understand the daily decisions that parents make to ensure their safety. Growing up in Jackson Heights, Queens, I could not understand my mother's extreme protectiveness or why she was so afraid whenever I went out, even to the corner store. I always thought it was because she did not trust me. I felt smothered and isolated in my new environment. From the extreme freedom I'd had until then, living in a tiny town in Colombia where children played on the streets until it was bedtime, I was suddenly confined to a small apartment with a television as my sole companion until my mother and brothers arrived home from work at night. I became a resentful adolescent and fed this resentment through comparisons of an almost bucolic life back home to a tragic captivity in a cement jungle, where no one cared about their neighbours. This, I thought, was the greatest calamity in my life.

It took me many years to understand the harsh reasons and the real significance of my mother's decision to migrate. In the end, it was I who reaped the greatest advantage out of all my siblings: I was the only one who was able to go to university and who never had to work as hard as they do. I had to make peace with the fact that this migration had been for my sake; that whatever identity crisis I chose to wallow in was not my mother's fault. I finally understood my mother's incredible strength and willpower to take that difficult step at the age of 40. When I turned that same age, I started to wonder if I would have been able to make that decision – if I would have had the courage and power to go to a foreign country to work for the sake of my children. My life has been so easy and carefree compared to my mother's; choosing not to have children or get married, I studied, travelled and lived in many different places, always convinced that I could do whatever I wanted. This was the result of my mother's sacrifice. Without it I would not have been able to choose this life for myself and make my dreams of freedom come true.

However, for my family the American dream was not so easily achieved. Caught between making ends meet and addicted to the American trend of compulsive buying, poor immigrants arrive to do the dirty work no one else wants. They want their children to have what they could not, but their children grow up in such abundance they rarely have a reason to want to study or work hard. I saw how this vicious cycle operated: the constant hard work was futile in the face of obsessive consumerism and credit card debt. It ruined the chances of achieving the American dream of owning one's home and being comfortable enough to work less.

I went away to study and escaped from that life and, as soon as I finished university, I announced to my family that I would return to Colombia for good. Would my mother have felt betrayed by this? I have never asked her. No one in the family believed me. They told me I would not get used to life there and would be back in no time. I stayed in Colombia and travelled to many countries, always returning to the US to visit my family since they could rarely afford to visit me. Of my parents and siblings, only my mother had been able to visit me in Bogotá. And that conversation in my apartment in 2008 made me question many things about my attitude to life. She revealed secrets, things which I did not know had happened between her and my father, such as the reason for their final breakup when they were already in their 60s. Being the youngest, I never witnessed the truly difficult moments my family went through. My brothers and sister had seen and experienced many hardships which I barely knew of, and they had sheltered me from this. That unforgettable talk with my mother made me feel such a connection to her despite our differences.

After the intense talk and the tears, I went alone to walk my dog. I started looking at the people in the park, children playing, dogs running, the trees, and the grass. I was feeling something that I could not identify. Slowly I understood that the feeling was utter comfort and tranquility. But the following thought was what stunned me: I could maintain this feeling. I could actually live continuously feeling this serenity. Why not? There was nothing lacking in my life. I did indeed have everything I wanted; my mother was healthy, my family was well despite their economic problems, I had shared 11 years of my life with a partner and we had made a comfortable home with a dog adding to the bliss. Was this not happiness? I remember hearing in some movie that happiness was not getting what you wanted but being satisfied with what you have. If I died at that moment, wouldn't I be able to say that I had lived a wonderful life?

This was such a strange revelation, strange because of its simplicity. Why did it take me so long to understand this? It must be true that wisdom comes with age. It took me 40 years to understand that the constant fears and anxieties – worrying about the future and what I don't have, or what I have and don't want to lose – were keeping me from enjoying my present. I resolved to stop my obsessive thinking and worrying and my pervasive need to have everything under control.

An epiphany at age 40. It all sounds pretentious now that I read over it. Nevertheless, it was an honest feeling at that moment. It gave me a resolution to strive for and provided an excuse and enough courage to start writing this story.

Double Entendre

Mark Yeow

As the air turns to panel-beaten steel the drones begin to
tread the streets, briefcase-banging in their thousands.
Grit and pork-ribs, 'Sale Sale Sale' the hangdog
tricolon of the new millennium. Doorways
neon, friedroadkill flapping morosely by the wayside,
too stale to vault the kerb.
By the old cinema, a rag-man kneels, head bowed,
as though to pray for man's salvation; that it might fall
into his collection-tin.

In the distance someone yells, 'Hey, here's a
riddle: What's long and black and hurts when it
goes off in your mouth?'

'Pearls and a pacifier please!'
Dress-Ups, Dolls and Donning Nanna's Dishy Couture

Bridie Connellan

At the ripe old age of five, the thought of throwing on my Nanna's unwanted sheer delphinium Sunday-best dress over an appropriate slip, teamed with matching duck-egg handbag and gigantor 'clop shoes' (aka heels for the underage), signalled the beginning of a golden weekend of delight, dreams and dinner parties. Like many kindergarten kids, the prospect of dress-ups heralded an afternoon of grown-up bliss interrupted only by the insistent calling of an evening meal.

By decorating ourselves with beads and bobbles worthy of any extravagant sugary tea and scones gathering, we essentially turned ourselves into warm-blooded Barbie dolls, embellishing our young selves with enough accessories to put our plastic patriot back on her shelf. As enlarged dolls ourselves, the addition of a parasol could only heighten the giggly delight which came from adorning our childish bodies with elements of 'grown-up gear', inspiring dreams of parlours and powder puffs; we were regular domestic goddesses. With the advantage of retrospect in an era of female lib, it almost seems quite unnerving that we were exhilarated by the chance to fashionably emulate the housewives of the 1940s in matching aprons and headbands ... but then again, their pearls were quite fetching.

It is no surprise that dress-ups were, and are, a predominantly girly realm of pearls, pinks and petticoats; however, it is far from fair of us to exclude the odd unfortunate brother from his curious delving in the world of fabulous hats and hairpieces, not to mention the occasional neighbouring boy who was capable of creating an outfit more fabulous than any of us.

What can I say, Tommy Thompkins just worked that fuchsia scarf and fluro visor ensemble better than me. Jerk.

High heels and flowing gowns were all novelties; symbols that represented a fantasy land in which tea and crumpets were the highlight of any truly elegant lady's day. And if materials were scarce, the humble dress-up even transcended physical garments with paper-dolls having their hey-day both in our childhoods and our mums' before us. Attaching pictorial clothing with tabs to hang on the shoulders of our 2D divas was one way to avoid the neighbours catching you in cocktail pink lipstick and a lacy bra over a frilly dress.

Essentially this fashionistic ritual all comes down to the magical world of make-believe, and our childlike penchant for exploring the endless realms of the imminent, impossible, immeasurable imagination. According to my mum the preschool teacher (who is totes better than yours, na-uh, I'm dobbing), dress-ups enable children to enact situations they have imagined or express emotions not commonly encountered in their life meanderings. Well, at five years of age I certainly didn't feel panicked by the thought of my closest girlfriends arriving within minutes of my crème brulee emerging from the oven! Golly gosh, fetch me a handkerchief to prevent my exquisite red lipstick and blue eyeshadow from running!

It saddens me that dress-ups today seem to be limited to thematic parties and the odd op-shopper who is brave enough to call that 50c magenta chenille sack dress their own for the afternoon. The opening of chests of glory that once signalled our transformation from five-year-olds to ladies of lake houses are now reserved for the weekends. The joys of themed 21sts are a relic of the sheer bliss of whisking oneself off to Characterville where the dress code of the real world need not apply. And even at the age of 20-something, who can deny the

51

exaltation of donning a sparkly tiara for the final countdown of the year? Three, two, one… Happy New Headgear!

Andy Baumgartner, a kindergarten teacher from Augusta, Georgia in the United States, cautions that it is crucial for us to nurture and build children's imaginations or they won't grow into adults who can think creatively about how to solve the world's problems. So perhaps, what the world needs now, is love, sweet love … of dress-ups. Perhaps government policy should stipulate a requirement of at least one wacky-tacky tie day per year to tide us over, at least for starters. Then perhaps (in my own scone and clop-shoe-filled mind) we could take some aesthetically pleasing steps towards rekindling that bliss we felt when donning a floral hat. Politicians in bonnets, judges in oversized shades, bartenders in fluro kimonos, teachers in tutus? How ridiculously merry would the legal system then be? Wishful thinking of such ecstatic emotions from childhood nostalgia, there is only one thing for a wardrobe idealist such as this youngster to do …

grow up.

Something I Didn't Know About You

Hannah Lee

I found your suicide note in the breast pocket of your favourite tweed jacket. It was wrapped by the chains of your gold pocket watch, smelling of tobacco and French cologne.

I came across the note by pure accident. Firstly, I followed your wife, Emily, back to your place after the funeral so that she could cry for 30 minutes and make some of her famous chamomile tea, which I hated. I sat with her for a little while, politely pretending to drink her tea and feeling rather awkward when your son, Jimmy, entered the kitchen to give her a hug. Now, you know I'm no good at comforting or cheering people up, so instead of awkwardly cupping my arms around the two mourners and saying, "There, there", I decided to take one last look at your study – the room where we'd shared many a conversation about work, wives and children. I know it was rude of me to just leave in the middle of this moving moment, but seeing as I know you and Emily so well, I decided Emily would see my up and leaving as a gesture of respect, leaving her and her son to have some time alone. Besides, I don't think she even noticed.

With a cautious glance back at the kitchen I was fleeing from, I tiptoed up the familiar staircase to your office. How many times had I visited your house? As your best friend, I had played golf with you multiple times and come back to your house for a cup of tea and a quick chat to your son while you and Emily had another of your thunderstorm-like fights. I can recall countless dinners where the food was warm, but the conversations cold. I've even slept in the guest room and woken to find you weak and high-strung from sleeplessness. I worried about you, dear old friend. I'd been there through everything. I couldn't believe that you had not called upon me when you were at your greatest level of despair.

"He's had a long history of depression."

"He'd been less talkative over the last few days."

"I could tell something was really bothering him, but I didn't want to ask him."

"My God, I can't believe he killed himself."

"Jumped right from the roof of his apartment building in broad daylight, he did."

"He must have left a suicide note somewhere. There must be proof that will clear this matter up."

I heard people talking about you everywhere. I felt like saying, "You idiots … you knew nothing about him … don't pretend you knew him." They acted all shocked and surprised when they heard the news. I was the only one who walked out of the funeral feeling the same as I had when I entered. I felt … indifferent.

Once I entered your study, I could instantly smell and feel the living you in the very room. The old photographs tacked to your billboard, your old pipe and vintage records from your college years – every single item in the room emanated your laugh, your embrace, your breath … I could swear I even felt your hands pressed into the very wood of your desk. Excited and energised by your presence in the room, I rifled my hands through your filing cabinet, ran my finger through the dust gathered on your shelf and rubbed my nose deep into the scent of your tweed jacket. That's when I felt the note in there with your pocket watch. At first I thought there'd be money in there – money I could use to buy a lemon tart and a bus ticket – but instead, I got a piece of paper and Grandpa's timekeeper. I swung the pocket watch in large gold loops of blur while reading your farewell letter. It read:

Dear Emily,

I love you. I love you. I love you.

Michael.

The moment I read it I didn't want to believe it, but the fact that you didn't want me around when you were going to kill yourself made my suspicions intensify. I threw myself up those apartment stairs. I couldn't even wait for the elevator to come down and tell me that my best friend had not *jumped* from the top of an apartment roof but *fallen*?! When I got to the roof, I kicked open the door and let the wind rush into my burning throat. Thirty flights of stairs and packet-a-day smoking do not enjoy each other's company. I stepped out onto the roof, the sun piercing into my eyes. The roof was bare, save for an apple crate propped up against the edge where you'd leapt and a discarded old watering can. I carefully walked to the edge where you would have stood. Hands on my hips, I didn't want to do it. I didn't want to find out what you'd been hiding from me.

I stepped up onto the apple crate that you had used as a stair to your death and leaned over the edge of the apartment roof. Hanging over the edge, hidden from view, was a hanging pot of chamomile flowers … you literally had to dangle over the edge to water them and see them.

"FUCK – YOU!"

I yelled it, loud as I could.

After such a long friendship, I'd been betrayed. You'd been diagnosed with me for years and now I find that your death was not the result of our time spent together, but an accident. Watering chamomile flowers over the roof of an apartment, away from damage and detection?!

You bastard. I could see you now, climbing up here behind my back and smiling to yourself, picturing Emily's face when she'd see these fresh chamomile flowers to use for her tea. God, I hate that tea.

I sat on the roof for a long time, just holding onto your little confession note that wasn't really a suicide note at all. I'd known you since you started work at the bank. I thought I knew you. I thought I knew how you felt about your wife, your work ... your life. I must have had the wrong person.

I unchained the pot in which the chamomile flowers sat and took them downstairs. It was already night time and Emily had fallen asleep with Jimmy in her arms. You know, I'd planned on staying here for another four months. I would have gotten to know Emily and Jimmy a little better in that time, but now I feel like I've exceeded my visitation hours. I placed the flowers on their apartment balcony and placed your note in the breast pocket of Emily's jacket before leaving. I guess you'll thank me for that.

See, even Depression has a heart.

Bittersweet Discovery

Pip Muratore

EVERYTHING IN THIS BOX £10.
It lies there, discarded, overlooked.
I can't help but pick it up and rifle through its pages,
yellowed with age and frayed at the edges.
How did it get here, this of all things?
Gazing back at me are the faces of past generations;
generations not of my flesh, but of another's –
the heritage and lineage of an unfortunate soul
forced to sell memories for a pittance,
a pathetic attempt to stave off debt
and eke out one more day of liberty
without fear of creditors or debt collectors.
The faces in the album almost appear to know,
their sad eyes following me as I thumb the pages.
They too knew poverty, and their children know it still.
Tragic, to part with something so dear,
yet worthless to any but the one who recognises the sitters,
who sees them as more than faded daguerreotypes from a dead epoch.
Still, my morbidity wins out over my sympathy.
I rifle around in my pocket and offer a note.
The transaction complete, I walk away
with someone else's family tucked under my arm.

Harmony at £3.95

Sam Lewin

One might remember (if one is me) Mr Walter Pater's reflections on *The Picture of Dorian Gray* as a catalogue of failed Epicureans; or rather, as an analysis of the faults of each particular character, regarding the aesthetic and even moral complexity, and most importantly harmony, that is essential to true Epicureanism. Although we apologise, repeatedly, to Mr Pater for not understanding Greek, surely even he must acknowledge the changes that have taken place regards our self-styled title: Epicurean. So he might help us then, as we look for, in our 'foodie' way, what constitutes true harmony.

Unlike Mr Wilde and his mentor and critic, many of us have had the misfortune of working in this horrible business, gastronomy, and we may fancy that we know something more about the true nature of modern food. It is well worth the time and mental real estate to commit to reading the very short *Dinners and Dishes*, a review by Mr Wilde of a book by that title. It reveals the preconceptions and attitudes of a man of aesthetic taste who, luckily, never dealt with the preparation of food. We do not share his blessed ignorance, and can hardly be blamed for our reluctance to choke down the most beautiful dish, when in our minds it is associated with a rather large and sweaty chef who steals chicken wings and uses his hair net to drain peas.

There is, no matter where one goes, a horrible sense of pretension in fine food. Like the workman who never sees a cathedral for the scaffolding, we have our noses held roughly against the stone (and pigeon leavings), and feel rather silly and at the same time sympathetic as everyone below points and is awed by religious beauty. Even monks must wear pyjamas, or something to sleep in, worst of all nothing to sleep in, and they would appear quite ridiculous to us in this condition. Carrying with us this horrible knowledge, and requiring *harmony* for proper Epicurean bliss, we must therefore find a) that which is edible and never ridiculous, or b) that which is inedible and always ridiculous. It is of course more acceptable to eat this very article than to eat paper masquerading as something else, for instance cereal or some supermarket meat, which vegetarians should feel quite comfortable sampling.

To find this first variety of food one must go to nature, where the equivalent of our human vulgarity is a purity of taste and nutrition. When I sleep at night I see a pastoral scene, in which a beautiful golden Madonna sits upon a ladder in stained overalls and surveys her country as she draws flavour from an orchard of oranges and pomegranates (I think I dream on the east of the Mediterranean). When I wake up I see advertisements for *Pom*, pomegranate juice, and I go to farmers' markets which have squeezed my beautiful orchard into Styrofoam boxes and which cultivate the nerves to try to sell it to me. As city dwellers we have this misfortune: that for us the cathedral is always covered in scaffolds, and the synesthesiastic bliss necessary to Epicureans is impossible to achieve. In all this noise who can really hear the orange? With all these flashing lights who can see the 613 seeds of the pomegranate explode in one's mouth? There is definitely no time for us to remember the symbolic and religious value of this; so in the end we aren't even looking at a cathedral with scaffolds, but simply a large box over which a spider has spun its web. This aside, there is one rule to which every considerate thinker should adhere: one cannot buy nature – and nor would one want to.

The solution then, is to be found where the inedible meets the hideous. Here there is no masquerade, there is no deception; in fact, one could argue, there is harmony. There is nothing but embarrassment in physical confrontation in the most expensive restaurants; but in a bar the fistfight has a certain rural charm, and reminds us forcibly of Australian bush-dancing, which is at least twice as painful. We yearn for a place where we stare across the counter at an ugliness of preparation that is reflected in our food, rather than hidden there, and in which, therefore, there is an anecdote rather than outrage. McDonald's has done more for Epicureanism than Epicurus, because the purity of our alliance against it makes us the greatest of friends. Yet its value is often understated. At the fast-food establishment we are informed by every sense that we are eating cardboard, not merely by our tastebuds. We can hear the sugar-sweetness of the burger roll in the screaming pleasantries of the next sale. Religious symbolism too, is not lost to this more base form of cookery, for in God's wrath at the fatal curiosity that brought us here, we are forced to dine on yellow pillars of salt that will, inevitably, kill us faster.

In writing this we recommend McDonald's as much as we recommend a fistfight, that is to say not at all. But the avid fistfighter hides today behind that horrid and delightful book *Fight Club*, and seeks therein a philosophical justification for his non-philosophical actions. As humans we need such narratives to define ourselves. As Epicureans, in particular, I hope that when we look into the fast-food restaurant we don't see a more primitive man, but rather one searching for true aesthetic bliss in food. McDonald's hurts more than a fist ever could, but I hope that Mr Pater and Mr Wilde, who live now in my orange and pomegranate orchard, might smile upon us as we walk up to a greasy counter, knowing that in doing so we are experiencing the vitality that must be lived in life, and that Mr Wilde must have felt when imagining Dorian's own fistfights. As Epicureans we owe this to ourselves, for without the grotesque, the sublime is merely superlative boredom.

The Emasculation of Divorced Dads

Monique Ewen

A survey of recent literature on families shows that, just as there is no culturally coherent way of dealing with divorce, there is also a lack of an established discourse for understanding men's experiences of divorce. Drawing on interviews with divorced fathers as well as Judith Butler's theory of gender and identity, I examine how men's experiences of divorce are affected by the construction of masculinity through performance. In particular, the stigmatisation of divorce through its construction as a deviation from normative discourses of heterosexuality and how melancholic loss is useful in understanding why men are so profoundly affected by divorce. To do this, I have looked at how the performance of gender through marriage is related to a man's sense of identity and self-worth, and examined what it is about marriage that imbues divorced men with profound feelings of failure and loss.

> I did not expect the separation. I was devastated. Suddenly I had no wife, no children, no home and very little money. I do not think it was for the best. I have lost everything: the love of my wife and the life of my son. I am unable to be the father I wanted to be. - Warwick[1]

> The hardest part of leaving home is leaving your territory, your wife and family, your identity. You feel like you've got nothing. There's a terrible emptiness. - Tim[2]

---

[1] Green, 1998, p.3.

[2] *Ibid.*, p.18.

Although I have not intended to exclude any particular party, I have focused primarily on divorced fathers because their experience most acutely illuminates both the establishment and breakdown of masculinity in relation to family and home life. My research has been informed by three interviews with divorced men from the group 'Dads in Distress' and also by my own experiences as the eldest daughter in a divorced family. Butler's theories of performativity and gender melancholia have provided the framework for my research; primarily an understanding of the way that gender is performed, constructed and reiterated in white western culture.

Research Methods

A discourse analysis was necessary for three main reasons. Firstly, men's experiences of divorce can be understood through the socially distributed and internalised stereotypes and assumptions that individuals embody. Secondly, I have found that there is a gap in theories of divorce where an understanding of men's experiences needs to be established. Thirdly, the interviews I have conducted were important not only in giving me a deeper insight into the issues faced by men, but also in illuminating the discourses that these men engage with in order to understand their own experiences.

The men I interviewed were contacted through the 'Dads in Distress' website. My sample was limited by the fact that not all fathers seek help. The men who attend 'Dads in Distress' are those who actively want to promote a better relationship with their children. It is also limited in the sense that, as Naomi Gerstel's research found, only about ten per cent of divorced people join groups, and those who don't join these groups stigmatise those who do as weak in some way.[3] Despite these limitations, the interviews were still useful in contributing to an understanding of men's feelings and experiences of divorce.

---

[3] Gerstel, 1987, p.184.

The interviewees were three middle-aged men of different working backgrounds, from different areas in Sydney. The circumstances surrounding each individual's divorce and family life varied greatly; including differences in the number of children and their age at the time of the divorce, the amount of contact allowed to the father, the length of the marriage and the reasons for the divorce, as well as the particulars of re-marriage. Despite these differences, the concerns of each of the men were very similar. The primary concerns were money and the children. However, I was wary of the tendency for these individuals to become preoccupied with financial issues because they are easier to discuss than personal and emotional issues.

In approaching the interviews I anticipated that the men would be hurt, angry and possibly looking for revenge or someone to blame. What I found instead was that these men felt confused and defeated. They wanted to talk, but they were also wary of being exploited and needed to know that they could trust me. I expected my own experience of divorce would inevitably affect and inform my research. However, I also found that the research informed my own experience and opened up new understandings that I had not previously considered.

Main Study

Marriage plays an integral part in the construction of identity in men's lives. It provides a framework that a man can either choose to accept or reject, thereby accepting or rejecting the normative performance of heterosexual masculinity. As Butler argues, "there is no gender that is 'expressed' by actions, gestures, speech, but that the performance of gender was precisely that which produced retroactively the illusion that there was an inner gender core".[4] In other words, a man's sex does not necessarily or reliably *determine* his masculinity;

---

[4] Butler, 1995, p.31.

rather, the performance of masculinity in a particular way becomes *being* masculine.

Marriage is essential to the normative performance of heterosexual masculinity. Steven Nock argues that there are very few public ways of marking the time when a boy becomes a man, and so marriage has become a central rite of passage into manhood.

> Normative marriage is the only way by which *most* males can become 'men' ... A man develops, sustains and displays his masculine identity in his marriage. The adult roles that men occupy as husbands are core aspects of their masculinity.[5]

It follows that, once attained, the loss of such a core aspect of masculinity would have a profound affect on a man's sense of identity and self-worth. Alice Chatillon's 1991 Ph.D. dissertation found that "separated men appeared to suffer more emotional distress, more loss of self-esteem and more damage to their identity than that experienced by separated females".[6] Hence, failure to perform one's gender through marriage is equated with failure to be a 'proper' person.

As Irvine and Klocke suggest, "By failing to maintain a relationship, they had failed a major test of adulthood".[7] This failure may well be compounded by what Butler argues is excluded from the performance of heterosexuality: that is, homosexual desire.

> In a man, the terror over homosexual desire may well lead to a terror over being construed as

---

[5] Nock, 1998, p.6.

[6] Chatillon, 1991.

[7] Irvine, & Klocke, 2001, p.31.

feminine, feminised, of no longer being properly a man, or of being a 'failed' man, or of being in some sense a figure of monstrosity or abjection.[8]

'Real' Men

Marriage is important for proving masculinity, for being a 'proper' man or a 'real' man. However, it is also important in the way that it *structures* masculinity. Dorothy Smith explains that there are governing processes in our society that are organised as distinct social entities and operate externally to those persons who participate in and perform them.[9] Men and women's ways of knowing themselves – including their expectations and experiences of marriage – are performatively predetermined. Traditionally, men's practices of knowing themselves as fathers and husbands have been 'to provide for' and 'to protect'. There is an inherent sense of social and moral responsibility in marriage.[10]

> He should be the father of his wife's children, he should be the provider for his wife and children, and he should protect his family. Accordingly, the male who refused to provide for or protect his family was not only a bad husband; he was somehow less than a man.[11]

In my interview with Matthew, he expressed this in terms of no longer being allowed to be a man. He said that what men lose in divorce is their right to take a role, to be involved in their families and to make decisions about their children's

---

[8] Butler, 1995, p.24.

[9] Although Smith's work is not directly about marriage and divorce, significant parallels can be drawn between her 1987 research into the social invalidation of the mentally ill and social invalidation of divorced people in society.

lives.[12] In other words, divorce excludes men from what they previously saw as their primary role and function. Thus it excludes them from their masculinity and positions them as devious.[13]

Ways of Knowing

Men's ways of knowing themselves as husbands and fathers is to rely on marriage as a way of structuring and regulating their behaviour. An expression of this can be found in Gray and Merrick's explanation of why men find it easier to deal with the legal issues of divorce than women. In divorce, the loss that women experience is the loss of the relationship and the attachment, whereas for men, the loss experienced is the loss of the institution of marriage – an institution that regulates and allows for their sense of commitment, responsibility and autonomy.[14]

The men I interviewed expressed a strong sense of marriage as a commitment and a responsibility: a way of belonging.

---

[10] From my own experience of divorce, I was recently discussing this project with my Dad and he said to me, "When I got married to your mother it was like the world changed. It was like when you were born the world changed. It's not something you can pinpoint but people's attitudes towards me were radically different."

[11] Nock, 1998, p.6.

[12] Personal communication, May 2008.

[13] Personal communication, May 2008. "I consider myself to be a man, a masculine man, and I love being a man. But because of this (at times the ridicule I faced and the questions going through court) I've felt that I was looked on as something less because I was a man. They made me feel as though my every thought was devious, and I couldn't make a decision unless it involved trying to manipulate my wife into inappropriate behaviour".

[14] Gray, & Merrick, 1996, p.245.

The divorce left them feeling defeated, lost and alienated.[15] Marriage was their way of binding themselves to their wife and children. Matthew explained that a woman carries a child in her womb for nine months and that gives her a very strong bond with the child, whereas for the father:

> ... there has to be some commitment, an emotional and psychological commitment. Marriage is a public acknowledgement that there's a commitment to this woman, these children and this household. That means a lot to a man.[16]

For these men, their faith in the marriage system compounds their shock at its failure, leaving them feeling betrayed, bewildered and totally unprepared to deal with the consequences of divorce.[17] They feel that the system has abandoned them and they find it difficult to renew their trust in people and society.[18] Matthew said: "you feel cheated".[19] As Peter explained:

---

[15] Personal communication, May 2008. "I gave up the whole idea of fighting for the children, or wanting custody, or proving that I was an OK dad. I didn't go down that track. I just said 'look this is my daughter, if you want to stay with your mum, that's your choice I'm not going to fight it.' So my opinion of it was that, sure I could have pursued it in court but what would it prove? And what would it really do? ... I think at that time I had a very poor self-esteem and view of myself as a father."

[16] Personal communication, May 2008.

[17] Personal communication, May 2008. "These dads think that they're going out to work everyday, bringing in the finances to give their family a good home, roof over their heads, food on the table ... Nine times out of ten, the dads when they're telling their story, the whole separation issue comes as a shock to them, and their comment is 'She knew exactly what she was doing, she had the police lined up and everything.' ... Everyone knows except them."

[18] Personal communication, May 2008. "It's really left me dead. I have serious trust issues now ... You feel betrayed – betrayal is a prominent word in the group [Dads in Distress] when the dads talk about their feelings."

[19] Personal communication, May 2008.

You don't get married thinking that you're going to
get divorced ... When you get married you think of
it as something that's complete, as an achievement
and going to work. And when it breaks up, it's
failed; you've failed. Your whole ambitions, your
whole idea of it, is gone by the way-side.[20]

Re-negotiating Relationships

In addition to the feelings of loss and bewilderment regarding
the performance of masculinity, a divorced man must also
renegotiate his position within his social networks. While
married, this position relies on, and is informed by, his status
as a married man. His relationships with his family and those
outside of it are mandated, outside of his knowledge, by the
social organisation of marriage in society.

Eve Sedgwick argues that men's relationships with other men
are always necessarily mediated through the presence of a
woman:

Patriarchal heterosexuality can best be discussed
in terms of one or another form of the traffic in
women: it is the use of women as changeable,
perhaps symbolic, property for the primary purpose
of cementing the bonds between men.[21]

Thus, it seems that marriage itself is a necessary presence in
the social organisation of men's relationships. Additionally,
research suggests that married men are likely to rely solely
on their wives for emotional support and intimacy;[22] that their
relationships with their children are often mediated through

---

[20] Personal communication, May 2008.

[21] Sedgwick, 1985, pp.25–6.

[22] Irvine, & Klocke, 2001; Candib, 1995.

their relationships with their wives;[23] and that their status as married males affects their position at work and within social groups.[24] Without their marriage men lose their familiar ways of functioning within their social network and, as a result, all of their relationships need to be redefined.

'Absentee Dads'

Over the last 20 years there has been a significant amount of research into post-divorce father absence.[25] The overwhelming conclusion is that divorced fathers have difficulty maintaining a close relationship with their children – not just because they have less contact with them – but also because they rely on the mother to mediate their relationship with their children.

Nehami Baum describes the situation of one father who, prior to divorce, was very involved in his children's lives. After the divorce, however, he was unable to maintain a relationship with them without also maintaining a relationship (however contentious) with their mother.[26] Baum explains that this man was unable to let go of his wife and marriage, and was therefore unable to define a new relationship with his children.

Nicholas Townsend has also conducted significant research into marriage, parenting and fatherhood. He argues that men see the concepts of 'wife and children' and 'marriage and family' as inseparable.

Men's relationships with their children are

---

[23] Baum, 2006; Townsend, 1999.

[24] Nock, 1998.

[25] For a start see Arendell, 1992; Baum, 2006; Kissman, 1997; Kruk, 1992; and Litton, & White, 1995.

[26] Baum, 2006, pp.251–253.

'mediated' through their relationships with the children's mothers. The mothers ... are placed by men in the position of orchestrating family life, including the kinds of interactions between fathers and children.[27]

The Stigma of 'Divorce'

It is clear then that men who get divorced face a complete redefinition of their masculinity and their social identity, and that this redefinition usually involves a strong sense of failure and loss. Gerstel argues that divorce itself has become more widely accepted but divorced people have not. The dividing of friends between the two spouses usually results in individuals feeling blamed for the divorce. Blame is attached to the individual rather than to the institution of marriage itself.[28]

However, this does not explain why divorce is still a problem in a wider social context. In the social circles of married couples, the divorced individual is seen as threatening and contagious.[29] "Many church people, community leaders, politicians and social commentators lament the 'broken home' and its dire consequences for society. They blame divorce for many problems of youth: delinquency, crime, suicide, drugs and alienation".[30] As Irvine and Klocke suggest, "Even if one does not take one's own divorce as a sign of failure, others often see it in that light. The process is still widely considered indicative of some personal flaw".[31]

---

[27] Townsend, 1999, p.92.

[28] Gerstel, 1987, p.177.

[29] Gerstel, 1987, pp.178–179.

[30] Green, 1998, p.36.

[31] Irvine, & Klocke, 2001, p.34.

This social stigmatisation of divorce was reflected in the interviews that I conducted. The men felt that they were ostracised for things that were out of their control. Things such as the assumption that they were 'mummy's boys' for having to move back home with their parents after the divorce for financial reasons;[32] or the assumption (mostly in the legal system) that because they were unable to be successful husbands they were also unable to be responsible parents.[33]

Although divorce may have become more widely accepted and blame more individualised, divorce is still a social problem. The reason for this may be found in Butler's theory of gender melancholia.

Gender Melancholia

Butler's theory attempts to make sense of the unseen psychological elements contributing to the way gender is constructed and performed. She proposes that heterosexuality is actually based on a foreclosure of homosexual attachment where the prohibition of homosexuality results in a double disavowal of both the attachment to and the loss of homosexual desire. This is what she calls a "melancholic loss" and it forms the primary basis for the construction of gender and identity. It results in a culturally pervasive denial that is repeated and ritualised throughout culture.

> What ensues is a culture of gender melancholy
> in which masculinity and femininity emerge as
> the traces of an ungrieved and ungrievable love,

---

[32] Personal communication, May 2008.

[33] Personal communication, May 2008. "It didn't matter whatever I'd suggest during that time, I found that it was always doubted. It didn't matter how much evidence I had, it didn't matter how much truth there was in my statement. The better my statement, the better my argument, the better I was at being deceitful."

indeed, where masculinity and femininity within the heterosexual matrix are strengthened through the repudiations they perform.[34]

Marriage acts to repudiate homosexuality. Marriage maintains the normative performance of gender, whereas divorce – in an unseen psychological sense – directly threatens our established ways of knowing and performing masculinity and femininity. In a society where marriage is *the* most important way of symbolically ratifying the performance of heterosexuality, divorce raises similar problems to homosexuality. Divorce is not only problematic because it makes us feel sad, but because it calls the very need for marriage into question; a need to repudiate homosexuality and thus confirm heterosexuality.[35]

Men are seen as the particular perpetrators of this problem because traditionally it is expected that men uphold and maintain the social order. In this light, divorced men have not only failed to appropriately perform their own gender, they have failed to uphold their social responsibility: to maintain the institutional organisation of gender through the repudiation of homosexual desire.

Conclusion

Marriage is essential in proving and structuring masculinity. It is integral to a man's sense of identity and self-worth. Consequently, divorce excludes men from their established practices of self-knowledge, automatically constructing them as either devious or failures. Divorce excludes men from what they previously perceived to be their primary role and function: to provide for and to protect their wife and family. It

---

[34] Butler, 1995, p.28.

[35] This may also explain the social problems with the marriage of gay and lesbian couples, as this would also call into question the concept of marriage as a confirmation of heterosexuality.

excludes them from their established ways of understanding themselves as men and alienates them from their established social practices.

Men are left feeling betrayed and bewildered at the prospect of having to renegotiate their masculinity in ways that they had previously taken for granted. This renegotiation occurs in the face of opposition from the legal system and from society in general. They remain engaged in a constant battle over how to negotiate a relationship with their children, not just in the court battles for custody, but also because of their reliance on the mother to mediate their relationship with the children. Divorced men face a complete redefinition of their masculinity and their social identity, and this usually results in a strong sense of failure and loss.

Perhaps the feminist discourses have been correct in arguing that men take too much for granted in family life. However, this also leaves them all the more unprepared to deal with the overwhelming self-redefinition that occurs as a result of divorce. These men need support and encouragement to become better men. Instead they face alienation, opposition and contempt.

Although divorce may have become more widely accepted, men and women still face disapproval and blame for their divorce. However, it is individual men who face the blame for failing to uphold the institutional organisation of gender through marriage. They face blame and alienation for threatening the normative discourses of heterosexuality. Thus it is men who need the most support, and unfortunately, it is also men who have the least access to support.

Bibliography

Arendell, T. (1992). 'After Divorce: Investigations into Father Absence', *Gender and Society*, 6(4):562–586.

Baum, N. (2004). 'On Helping Divorced Men to Mourn Their Losses', *American Journal of Psychotherapy*, 58(2):174–85.

Baum, N. (2006). 'Postdivorce Paternal Disengagement: Failed Mourning and Role Fusion', *Journal of Marital and Family Therapy*, 32(2):245–54.

Butler, J. (1995). 'Melancholy Gender/Refused Identification', In M. Berger, B. Wallis & S. Watson (Eds), *Constructing Masculinity*. London and New York: Routledge.

Chatillon, A.C. (1991). 'The Self-in-Relation Model and Sex Differences in Reaction to Marital Termination', Ph.D. Dissertation. Illinois: Loyola University of Chicago.

Gerstel, N. (1987). 'Divorce and Stigma' *Social Problems*, 34(2):172–186.

Gray, C. & Merrick. D.S. (1996). 'Voice Alterations: Why Women Have More Difficulty Than Men in Dealing with the Legal Process of Divorce', *Family and Conciliation Courts Review*, 34(2):240–251.

Green, M. (1998). *Fathers After Divorce*. Sydney: Finch Publishing.

Irvine, L. & Klocke, B. (2001). 'Redefining Men: Alternative Masculinities in a Twelve-Step Program', *Men and Masculinities*, 4(27):27–48.

Kissman, K. (1997). 'Noncustodial Fatherhood: Research Trends and Issues', *Journal of Divorce and Remarriage*, 28 (1–2):77–88.

Kruk, E. (1992). 'Psychological and Structural Factors Contributing to the Disengagement of Noncustodial Fathers After Divorce', *Family and Conciliation Courts Review*, 30(2):81–101.

Litton, F. & White, B. (1995). 'Noncustodial Fathers Following Divorce', *Marriage and Family Review*, 20(1 – 2):257–272.

Myers, M. (1989). *Men and Divorce*. New York: The Guilford Press.

Nock, S. L. (1998). *Marriage in Men's Lives*. New York and Oxford: Oxford University Press.

Personal communication with volunteer participants, May 2008. Names have been changed.

Sedgwick, E. (1985). *Between Men: English Literature and Male Homosocial Desire*. New York: Columbia University Press.

Smith, D.E. (1990). *The Conceptual Practices of Power: A feminist sociology of knowledge*. Boston: Northeastern University Press.

Townsend, N. (1999). 'Fatherhoods and Fieldwork: Intersections Between Personal and Theoretical Positions', *Men and Masculinities*, 2(87):87–97.

Townsend, N. (2002). *The Package Deal: Marriage, Work and Fatherhood in Men's Lives*. Philadelphia: Temple University Press.

Women in the Sin Bin

Ruby Prosser Scully

Matthew Johns: unless you've been hiding under an assessment rock, the name should trigger images of distraught young women, oafish rugby players and the sound of guilt-ridden apologies. Sex is always a touchy subject, and with the amount of scandal and media outrage, people are quick to jump on the bandwagon decrying celebrity morality and the poor role models they proffer. It's easy to point the pitchfork and light the torches for a good old-fashioned witch-hunt, but who's going to have your back when a bit of harmless gang-banging goes awry?

With people slinging issues of morality all over the media, it is important to first establish the facts of the matter (at least in line with my soapbox). As it stands, Johns, a team mate and a consenting 19-year-old barmaid had sex after a few drinks, and were later joined in the room by several other players for a bit of naked tackling practice.

Given the police didn't charge any of the players, I'm going to stick with the oft-forgotten adage of 'innocent until proven guilty'. To some, all this talk of 'consent' is irrelevant to the underlying oppression and victimisation of women in Australian society. To some, it seems so distasteful for any woman to be involved in group sex that it should be obvious that it was degrading and humiliating for the woman. These arguments assume she gave consent, and yet still lambast the men involved is astounding. Has nothing changed?

In the scramble to get Johns' head on a plate, the very people purporting to be women's rights activists powerfully reinforced gender stereotyping and dismissed the possibility that women should be held responsible for their actions. Talk of consent is thrown out the window when we have journalists like Adele Horin arguing that a man should be convicted of all rape charges unless he can prove he sexually satisfied the woman. Former sex-discrimination commissioner Pru Goward vehemently argued that the barmaid consented to sleeping with Mathew Johns, but assumed she wouldn't have consented to group sex on the highly subjective grounds of, "What woman would want that?"

Which makes me wonder – when will women start to take responsibility for their own sexual choices? Why are we still being told that a woman's sexuality is somehow weak, or non-existent? Let me give you a moment to reflect on the last time you witnessed a sexually aggressive woman. Maybe she was somebody you knew. Maybe she was you. It's outrageous to think: should any woman choose to take a guy home any given Saturday night, the responsibility is on his shoulders. Women have been encouraged to reclaim some ownership over their sexuality. An entire industry of glossy women's magazines is dedicated to publishing tips on how to have better sex, how to be more sexually liberated and open-minded, how to be an assertive, independent woman. And yet, it seems in light of this current media circus what we are observing is the Quantum Theory of Consent: if a woman gives consent and nobody sees it, did it really happen?

We've moved on from the quaint idea that sex must be within a religious or state-supported union to be legitimised and we're better for it. There are people out there who enjoy sex with men, or women, or both and perhaps even all at once, and more power to them. However, when judgmental words like 'slut' and 'whore' are still being spat at women who deviate from 'sexual norms', it's no wonder that this barmaid felt ashamed.

On the other hand, Johns' career, his family, and his club are all close to ruin. It seems his redemption will come at a price. During the wrap up of the *A Current Affair* report with Tracy Grimshaw, the media were insistent on getting a quote from Johns that served as a warning for future players. Presumably, what the morally outraged audience are looking for is a condemnation of group sex, and further apologies for the 'sexual exploitation' of young and 'vulnerable' females.

Without complete ownership over our bodies and our decisions, women will never have independence or equality. If there has been anything worth learning from the entire media circus, it is that calling a man a rapist to absolve a woman of responsibility proves a hard burden of debilitating consequences for all concerned.

Gettier's Problem

Michael Barnes

Edmund Gettier knocked on the Pearly Gates. He smiled quietly to himself. Edmund's smile resembled a particularly fine-polished ebony keyboard without the black bits, an electric keyboard, a truly electric smile. He had good reason to be pleased with himself. On earth he had been an American, a philosopher and a professor, in that order. During a long lifetime starting way back in 1927, to phrase it in the vernacular, he had 'done it easy'. While fellow philosophers like Jurgen Habermas and Roland Barthes had spent *their* extended lifetimes turning out tome after endless learned tome on God-knows-how-many philosophic conundrums, and Bertrand Russell had not only written all his own stuff but had also compiled a monumental summary of the thoughts of all the other important Western philosophers, he, Edmund Gettier, had written a scant three pages and had achieved immortality. His three pages had become known as "The Gettier Problem" and had been discussed, argued over, enlarged upon, castigated and praised for almost half a century. Edmund had written it merely in order to secure his job and it had resulted in him becoming a philosophic celebrity. No wonder he smiled. He ran over his very satisfactory life in his mind as he delivered another sharp rap on the Pearlies.

The gate was opened abruptly by a tall, slim man with a pencil-thin moustache of the type preferred by film actors and con-men in the 1940s. He looked vaguely familiar.

"Don't I know you?" Gettier asked, flashing the full set of upper and lowers. He spoke in the nicely rounded tenor of a Baltimore man polished by many years in academia.

The gatekeeper scowled and answered in the staccato tones of a New Jersey jerk, sharpened by years in vaudeville:

"Look, buddy, let's cut all the wise-guy cackle. I'm Bud Abbott. A guy your age musta seen me in the movies with that no-good bum Costello. Why is it always the little fat guy who gets all the laughs?"

Gettier smiled upon Abbott. "Are you asking this as a philosophical question?"

Abbott favoured Gettier with a piercing narrow-eyed glare "Let's get one thing straight from the start: I'm the straight man here. In fact, that's why I'm minding the gate."

Gettier grinned him down and said: "Let us consider three possibilities:

"Either Costello gets all the laughs because he is funny or because Abbott is in Rio;

"Either Costello gets all the laughs because he is funny or Abbott is in London;

"Either Costello get all the laughs because he is funny or Abbott is incontinent.

"Now let us examine each of these propositions and see whether we have true knowledge, which, as you know, has been widely defined since Plato's time as a justified true belief."

The gatekeeper glowered and replied: "Okay, wise-guy, you wanta play word games, we'll play word games. You know anything about baseball?" Before Edmund could respond, Abbott fired on like a machine gun: "We're at the Rose Bowl, see, the Yankees are fielding. And I can tell you Who's on first base, What's on second and I Don't Know's on third."

Edmund was beginning to enjoy himself. He loved baseball, he loved word games. "Okay," he agreed, "Who's on first?"

"Yes," said Abbott.

Their encounter then went like this:

Gettier: "I mean, what's the fellow's name?"

Abbott: "Who."

Gettier: "The guy on first base."

Abbott: "Who."

Gettier: "The first baseman."

Abbott: "Who."

Gettier: "The guy playing."

Abbott: "Who is on first."

Gettier: "I'm asking you who's on first?"

Abbott: "That's the man's name."

Gettier: "That's whose name?"

Abbott: "Yes."

Gettier: "Well go ahead and tell me."

Abbott: "That's it."

Gettier: "That's who?"

Abbott: "Yes."

Edmund Gettier's electric smile was beginning to fade. Their conversation seemed to have gone haywire. He suspected he was being ridiculed. He rattled on while still trying to manage a vestige of his smile.

"Let's get back to Plato," he suggested, "and see if we can get a justified true belief as to who is on first."

"He is," answered Abbott but Edmund quickly talked him down. "Consider these three propositions," he began.

"Either someone is on first or it is snowing in Copenhagen;

"Either someone is on first or it raining in Portugal;

"Either someone is on first or the cat is in the microwave.

"Now, can we deduce from this who is on first?"

Abbott: "You said it, buddy."

Gettier: "I said what?"

Abbott: "No, What is on second."

Gettier: "Can't we stick to the subject ...?"

Abbott: "The Subject is in the outfield."

Gettier's smile had vanished. He was beginning to get frustrated. He said with forced civility: "I'm not concerned about the outfield at this stage. I just want to know who is on first?"

Abbott was about to say "Yes", but he had become bored with the whole thing. He sighed: "I'm not worried about the snow in Copenhagen, the rain in Portugal or the cat in the microwave. They don't appear to be in any way connected to me. If you want to come in, you've got three choices. Either you can bunk in with Mr Wittgenstein who likes to discuss language issues, or with Mr Socrates who enjoys cross-examining his associates, or with Mr Roth."

"Which Mr Roth might that be?" Edmund inquired.

"It's Mr Roth the novelist," Abbott explained. "He wrote a book called *Portnoy's Complaint*. It's about wanking." Abbott paused for a moment.

"Come to think of it, I'll put you with Mr Roth. You two guys will enjoy talking to each other."

Abbott opened the Pearly Gates and let Edmund Gettier inside.

Dandelions

Veronica Wagner

They sprung up one midnight
Like a daydream and made the morning
Suddenly everything

A lifetime of birthdays
And everybody from miles around

Trumpeted around with party hats on
Leaping into them and carousing and tumbling
And everyone's clothes were fluffy and glorious

We picked enormous fluttering bouquets
Of dandelions, and proposed to sweethearts
And everyone was married

We lay down in it like a snowfield
As the white hive eddied around us merrily

Shadows slid longer and the thrill
Started to soften until everything
Was washed in orange-pink light

And we rested in our doorways
And watched them float like souls into heaven

But eventually every angel among them
Was gathered and lost or else blown into space

Until from me to the edge of night
Was an ocean of empty bodies.

Dada: A Nihilistic Gesture

Michelle Lee

> The only really ugly things are Art and anti-Art.
> Wherever Art appears, life disappears.[1]
>
> Francis Picabia

Francis Picabia's quote perfectly captures the true essence of the Dada era; with the discrediting of artworks came a cultivation of the gesture, a way of life. Dada was not about creating works of art in the traditional sense. Rather, it was a campaign to flout conventions in deliberately outrageous ways, intended to reveal the essential meaninglessness of modern life and to shock viewers into re-examining and re-evaluating their world. Through sardonic forms of art the Dadaists protested against the political propaganda of World War I and embraced spontaneity in all aspects of their art and lives, as a way of freeing themselves from a constraining definition of the artist and the art-object. In this sense, the Dadaist questioning of aesthetic values evoked a nihilistic gesture.

In order to understand Dada one must comprehend the state of mental tension in which it evolved. In February 1916, Hugo Ball founded the Cabaret Voltaire in Zurich. It was a cross between a nightclub and an art society, planned as a "centre for artistic entertainment"[2] with the intention that young artists would "bring along their ideas and contributions".[3] Ball became the "human catalyst who united around himself all the elements which finally produced Dada".[4] A group composed of

---

[1] Ades, 1983, p.117.

[2] Richter, 1997, p.16.

[3] *Ibid.*

[4] *Ibid.*, p.13.

refugees from World War I, "repelled by the slaughterhouses of the world war",[5] quickly formed, turning to art to express their anger over the system that had been its catalyst. Art was their means of protest against the traditions in art, society, and politics that had led to the horrors of the war. Dada's nihilistic and anarchic attitudes are further epitomised in the name 'Dada'. 'Dada' had no previous artistic significance and held different meanings in different languages, such as 'hobby-horse' in French. The irrelevant nature of the movement's name consciously describes the Dadaists' perception of the purposelessness of European life and culture.

However, the Dadaists believed in the power of elementary art to "save mankind" from political abominations. They believed that "by changing the order of language, art could reform the order of experience and so alter the conditions of social life".[6] This attitude is evident in Ball's theatrical and improvised performances of *Verse ohne Worte* (verse without words). These performances involved reciting incomprehensible sound poems, such as "gadji beri bimba, glandridi lauli lonni cadori".[7] The primitivism of the sound-based poetry reflects the Dadaist spontaneous, automatic and improvisatory approach to forming a social 're-beginning'. The alien nature of an unrecognisable, unintelligible 'non-language' evoked a utopian dream of an ideal realm, purified and abstract, whilst maintaining a critical reflection on a degraded world, almost as an involuntary expression of its brutalised condition.[8]

One of the essential preoccupations of Dada was an indictment of literature through its own literature. Dadaist literature

---

[5] Hughes, 1981, p.61.

[6] *Ibid.*

[7] Demos, 2005, p.7.

[8] *Ibid.*, p.8.

"stresses impulse and spontaneity".[9] Tristan Tzara's *Dada Manifesto 1918* marks the beginning of a new phase for Dada through its aggressive and nihilistic manner.[10] In the *Manifesto*, Tzara calls for spontaneity in art to free artists through a reduction of everything to an initial simplicity. Ultimately, Tzara argues that when literature is understood, it is "insipid".[11] The Dadaists wanted logic to be reduced to a minimum, while the reasoning or 'literature' should be primarily intended for the artist who creates the art. Thus, they wanted to see "the intensity of a personality transfer directly and clearly into the work"[12] in a way that purely illustrated the relationship between the artist and his or her vitality.

Dada stood for "exacerbated individualism, universal doubt and aggressive iconoclasm"[13] that had "no programme"[14] to fulfil. As Tzara states, "The beginnings of Dada were not the beginnings of art, but of disgust".[15] Dada was a protest, "a state of mind"[16] and a gesture of the soul. However, it is essential to grasp that Dada was never an art style, as the other Modernist movements, (such as Cubism) were; nor did it begin with a pugnacious socio-political programme, like Futurism. Dada stood for eclectic freedom to experiment, enshrining play as the highest human activity, and chance as

---

[9] Kristiansen, 1968, p.3.

[10] Ades, 1983, p.117.

[11] Tzara, 1993, p.129.

[12] *Ibid.*, p.387.

[13] Short, 1994, p.8.

[14] Richter, 1997, p.34.

[15] Rublin, 1982, p.12.

[16] Ades, 1983, p.111.

its main tool.[17] Accident and spontaneity played an important role in many of the improvisations at the Cabaret Voltaire.

The Dadaist focus on spontaneity and experimentation with new social forms and radical languages was also elaborated in the collages of Hans (Jean) Arp. For Arp, Dada meant the destroying of "the reasonable deceptions of man"[18] by recovering "the natural and unreasonable order".[19] Arp developed a new working method in his art forms known as the 'law of chance'. Arp assembled his collages by tearing up paper and letting the pieces drop without any conscious intervention onto a sheet of paper. Arp discovered that it conveyed "an expressive power that the original [consciously arranged collage] had failed to do".[20] This is evident in Arp's *Collage arranged according to the laws of chance.* Through the use of this discovery of powerful unfathomable chance, Arp wanted his art to give a "free flow to what was elemental and spontaneous".[21] Crucial to Arp was that these collages were impersonal and unaltered in their initial phase. However, a second stage was involved, in which Arp consciously altered the chance configuration of his materials until they achieved a level of completion satisfactory to him. Thus, the process entailed two separate and distinct stages; the first of random or 'chance' occurrence, the second of conscious formal resolution.[22]

However, it is problematic to assume that the title 'nihilist' can be attributed to all of the Zurich Dadaists. There were two distinct kinds of emphasis within Dada. There were the

---

[17] Hughes, 1981, p.61.

[18] Ades, 1983, p.114.

[19] *Ibid.*

[20] Waldman, 1992, p.133.

[21] *Ibid.*

[22] *Ibid.*

mystical and constructive-minded figures of Ball and Arp who were looking for a new art to replace an outworn and irrelevant aestheticism, and there were those like Tzara who were increasingly nihilistic and intent on destruction through mockery. Zurich Dada was "less egotistical with a naïve attitude, seeking recourse to primitive, automatic, universal forces, rather than individual exasperation".[23]

The experience of geopolitical displacement was central to Dada's identity.[24] Since Dada was essentially a mental attitude, efforts to determine its original appearance at one particular time and place have mostly been performed in vain. A good case can be made for New York, where the Dada spirit was unmistakably active well before its official baptism in Zurich.[25] This was highlighted by Hans Richter who wrote:

> We in Zurich remained unaware until 1917 or 1918 of a development which was taking place, quite independently, in New York. Its origins were different, but its participants were playing essentially the same anti-art tune as we were.[26]

New York Dada owed its beginnings to the arrival of Francis Picabia and Marcel Duchamp from Europe in June 1915. They were united in their determination to 'unlearn' painting; to challenge the assumptions that underpinned the institution of art in the West, even that of the avant-garde, and thus question the very principles of the creative act.[27]

---

[23] Short, 1994, p.32–34.

[24] Demos, 2005, p.9.

[25] *Ibid.*, p.22.

[26] Richter, 1997, p.81.

[27] Short, 1994, p.22.

Duchamp broke with artistic tradition by challenging the role of the artist. He was interested in the concept rather than the aesthetics of art. In this sense, Duchamp asserted that the artist's art-making practice and decisions, as to what constituted their art, did not have to adhere to conventional definitions of materials, technique, practice or the art-object itself.

Through humorous yet also nihilistic gestures, Duchamp's notorious 'ready-made' *Fountain* introduced a new broader conception of what art could be. Duchamp reasoned that there was no point in adhering to the principles, traditions, or values of art. *Fountain*, a porcelain urinal signed 'R. Mutt', is therefore a quintessential embodiment of Dada. On one level, Duchamp's *Fountain* is simply a visual joke. When he first submitted it as a sculpture to a New York City art exhibition in 1917 it was rejected on the grounds that a urinal could not be considered art. *Fountain* violates most traditional ideas about sculpture. Its apparent subject matter is so far removed from the usual realm of subject as to be shocking, even disgusting, to most audiences. Furthermore, Duchamp was not personally involved in creating or even supervising the fabrication of this piece. Instead of creating this sculpture, Duchamp 'found' it already made. Thus, it became apparent that what made *Fountain* a sculpture rather than a piece of plumbing was the fact that this particular urinal had been chosen by Duchamp for exhibition. Because he was a professional artist he argued that his act of selecting and then designating this object as 'art' transformed it into precisely that. In this sense, Duchamp's 'ready-made' was sketching out "possibilities of ever new impossibilities".[28]

---

[28] Spies, 1982, p.134.

Dada served a more politically charged purpose in Berlin.[29] The effect of the war on Berlin formed a stark contrast to the social and economic stability of Zurich. Richard Huelsenbeck noticed upon his arrival in 1917 that "In Zurich the international profiteers sat in the restaurants with well-filled wallets and rosy cheeks".[30] Whereas war-torn Berlin was a "city of tightened stomachers ... where ... men's minds were concentrating more and more on questions of naked existence".[31] The Expressionists had already provoked a fierce anti-war protest in German art, resorting to the view of the "self or the void; ecstasy or chaos".[32] However, the German Dadaists "rejected the Expressionist's cult of inwardness, urging that the soul only revealed its true qualities in action".[33] Thus, the 1918 *Berlin Dada Manifesto* was a sustained attack on Expressionism:

> The highest art will be the one which in its conscious contents presents the thousandfold problems of the day...
>
> Have the expressionists fulfilled our expectation of an art that burns the essence of life into our flesh?
>
> NO! NO! NO!
>
> Hatred of the press, hatred of advertisement, hatred of *sensations* are typical of people who prefer their armchair to the noise of the street.[34]

---

[29] Kranzfelder, 1994, p.32.

[30] Huelsenbeck, 1967, p.39.

[31] *Ibid.*

[32] Hughes, 1981, p.68.

[33] Short, 1994, p.38.

[34] Hughes, 1981, pp.68–71.

To underpin this polemic message while giving art its sense of urgency, the Berlin Dadaists invented 'photomontage'; a collage-like method, incorporating everyday visual materials, such as newspaper headlines, photographs and advertisements, "stuck on one another in ways that resembled the laps and dissolves of film editing".[35] These images could combine the grip of a dream with the documentary 'truth' of photography, revealing, what Raoul Hausmann described as "a visually and conceptually new image of the chaos of an age of war and revolution".[36] The Dadaists utilised photomontage to bring together disparate elements of contemporary Berlin in a way that made a sardonic comment on the culture from which they originated. By maintaining aspects of the parts' original meanings within the new meaning of the whole, conglomerate image, subversive cultural comment was the resulted of apposite juxtaposition. In this way, the Berlin Dadaists achieved the immediate critical impact that was missing from the culturally neutral assemblages of Dadaists such as Arp.[37] It became an effective method for making pronouncements about society as it remained in keeping with their anarchic ideas, especially with their notion of dispensing with traditional art.[38]

John Heartfield's work formed the most aggressive political use of photomontage. Heartfield's works take advantage of photography's 'reality-effect', "a kind of truth of which painting is not capable of",[39] in order to undermine the apparent reality and create images of otherwise invisible social facts. For instance, Heartfield's photomontage *Adolf, the superman:*

[35] *Ibid.*

[36] Short, 1994, p.42.

[37] *Ibid.*

[38] Waldman, 1992, p.112.

[39] Hughes, 1981, p.73.

swallows gold and spouts junk unmasks the corrupt reality of the Führer. Hitler's illegitimate and immoral connection to big business is portrayed through the swallowed gold coins visible inside Hitler's body. In this sense, Heartfield's photomontage explicitly demonstrates photography's potential to represent reality.[40]

The First International Dada Fair in Berlin in 1920 proved to be the climax of the movement. Suspended from the ceiling of the main gallery was a stuffed dummy dressed in a German officer's uniform and fitted with the head of a pig; close-by was a dressmaker's dummy with a lit electric light bulb for its head. Many of the works were clearly intended to protest against the German military and the German nation post-World War I.[41] The light bulb is framed in the most negative way as a comment on "the ignorant, the bestial, the grotesque side of man".[42] Furthermore, through the use of ordinary objects, such as a dressmaker's dummy, the Berlin Dadaists created a scathing indictment of society.

Through the art of satire, Berlin Dada principally targeted the institutions and mentality of the bourgeoisie. The Berlin Dadaists delighted in exposing the fraudulent ways in which the new Republic was dressing-up the old exploitive structures in 'democratic' clothes.[43] George Grosz created the most radical sourness and critique of the times. It was not painting but mankind that he detested. Grosz rallied against the conformity of Weimar politics: the canting patriotism of

---

[40] Levi, 1998, p.62.

[41] Waldman, 1992, p.108.

[42] Ibid., p.112.

[43] Short, 1994, p.42.

the empty speeches and sloganeering, the promises of a better future to a generation half-destroyed in the Great War.[44]

Overall, Dada came to stand for rebellion, disruption and change. Through a condemnation of the social, economic and political structure of the age, Dada attacked the prevailing culture. Contemptuous assaults on conventional and logical norms ranged from humorous absurdity to savage satire. The Dadaist anarchic attitude deliberately ignored the accepted techniques and subject matter of traditional art forms, aiming instead at the deliberate destruction of the achievements of Western culture. Although Zurich Dada is seen to form a less aggressive attack on the social situation than Berlin Dada, it was nevertheless pivotal in establishing the nihilistic ideologies that subsequently served Dada more profoundly in the anti-aesthetic gestures of New York Dadaists.

---

[44] Hughes, 1981, p.75.

Bibliography

Ades, D. (1983). 'Dada and Surrealism', In N. Stangos (Ed), *Concepts of Modern Art*. London: Thames & Hudson Ltd.

Canaday, J. (1959). *Mainstreams of Modern Art*. London: Thames and Hudson.

Demos, T.J. 'Zurich Dada: The aesthetics of exile', In L. Dickerman & M. S. Witkovsky (Ed), *The Dada Seminars*. Washington: National Gallery of Art.

Duchamp, M. (1996). 'The Creative Act', in K. Stiles & P. Selz (Ed), *Theories and Documents of Contemporary Art: a Sourcebook of Artists' Writings*. Berkeley: University of California Press.

Huelsenbeck, R. (1967). 'En Avant Dada: a History of Dadaism (1920)', In R. Motherwell (Ed), *The Dada Painters and Poets: an Anthology*. New York: George Wittenborn Inc.

Hughes, R. (1981). *The Shock of the New*. London: British Broadcasting Corporation.

Johnson, E.H. (1976). *Modern Art and the Object: a Century of Changing Attitudes*. London: Thames and Hudson.

Kranzfelder, I. (1994). *George Grosz 1893–1959*. Cologne: Benedikt Taschen.

Kristiansen, D. M. (1968). 'What is Dada?', *Educational Theatre Journal*, (20)3:457–462.

Levi, N. (1998). '"Judge for yourselves!" – the "Degenerate Art" Exhibition as Political Spectacle', *October*, 85:41–64.

Lucie-Smith, E. (1997). *Visual Arts in the Twentieth Century*. New York: Harry N. Abrams Inc.

Marzona, D. & Grosenick, U. (Ed), (2005). *Conceptual Art*. Cologne: Taschen.

Meecham, P. & Sheldon, J. (2000). *Modern Art: A Critical Introduction*. London: Routledge.

Meyer, U. (1972). *Conceptual Art*. New York: Clarke, E.P. Dutton & Co. Inc.

Motherwell, R. (Ed), (1967). *The Dada Painters and Poets: An Anthology*. New York: George Wittenborn, Inc.

Richter, H. (1997). *Dada: Art and Anti-Art*. London: Thames & Hudson Ltd.

Rublin, W.S. (1982). *Dada, Surrealism and their Heritage*. New York: The Museum of Modern Art.

Short, R. (1994). *Dada and Surrealism*. Hong Kong: Laurence King Publishing.

Smith, B. (Ed), (1974). *Concerning Contemporary Art: the Power Lectures 1968–1973*. Oxford: Oxford University Press.

Spies, W. (1982). *Focus on Art*. New York: Rizzoli International Publications Inc.

Tzara, T. (1993). 'Dada Manifesto 1918', In R. Huelsenbeck (Ed), *Dada Almanach*. London: Atlas Press.

Waldman, D. (1992). *Collage, Assemblage, and the Found Object*. London: Phaidon Press Limited.

Willet, J. (1978). *Art and Politics in the Weimar Period: the New Sobriety 1917–1933*. New York: Pantheon Books.

Fashion Me

Daniel Sleiman

The streets are an interesting place to sit and construe, wander and understand the society you reside in. It is filled with people of varying backgrounds speaking unintelligible languages, including English. Some are dressed fashionably. Or more appropriately, are fashioned by their dress. Others are banal looking or just plain uninteresting from a perceptive distance.

Fashion is a sociological classification. It is commonly acknowledged that people judge others by what they wear, even implicitly. Why do we do this?

Firstly it gives us a reference point, and fulfils ideas of our own sense of knowledge. Secondly it dictates our opinions about what we like and dislike and, in a sense, lets us know who we are. It is like conversing with a diverse range of people, without uttering a word. These conversations reflect our personality and how we represent ourselves to others. One might state ambivalence on certain issues or be completely frivolous. Being ambivalent is like wearing un-matching shoes and being frivolous is like wearing haughty colours. The misperception is of course real. Notwithstanding a great fashion sense, recognised by those I call the "fashionists".

The "fashionists" are appointed, often self-appointed, trend-setters. They design clothing for mass consumption and reside in a world of glamour. They have followers around the globe who conform to their idea of fashion and, as such, validate it. The "fashionists" can look at you and tell you what you are about. That is, your sexual orientation, your diet, your fears, your dreams, even why you think you look good wearing what you are wearing. They are like psychologists; but without those nerdy scientific connotations. All this makes no difference, or perhaps all the difference. The next time you get dressed make sure you know what you are getting into.

Dog

Amelia Dale

Life is rough rough. Only two months old – do you hear me? And I'm having a howl of a time. I might come from a dingo and the bitch in the farm to your left, but that doesn't make my tail less waggy, my fur less soft or my tongue less pink and pant-pant panting. I should be a-rolling and a-roaring in the dirt but I can barely move for hunger's tearing cat's teeth into my tummy's lining. Look, I'll roll over. Can you see my ribs? Yeah, you can tickle me if you want. But some food would be nice. Oh sure, it's a lovely day, the sun is a slick of petrol blazing in this lovely carpark of a sky but it's not so lovely that you might give this mutt a scrap of meat, eh? If pity were meat we'd all be neck deep in steaks, but instead you leave me here, empty belly burning in the scorching air, my puppy paws flailing, my young life wasting. I'll just roll in this dead magpie. At least now my carcass shall be fittingly perfumed with death and dark feathers, instead of stinking of algae and blackberries like everything else.

Nothing else grows on this tiny property but bloody blackberries. It's not a proper farm. Has no chickens or cows or sheep – mmm sheep. A couple over there picks blackberries. But wouldn't give any to me, no, no. Much too intent on each other to pity me.

The most tempting clumps of berries are closest to the muddy water where the guy shows off to the girl and now he's about to fall completely into the creek. He curses, he squeals, he holds out his arms to her, yells, "Anne!" and in the process flings his bowl up into the humid air.

Meanwhile, two fat old women are walking by the swamp-side and I'm prancing by their side.

"Think they make a cute couple?" says the woman who smells of meat pies and hair conditioner.

"While it lasts. She's no angel. Watch it, you're about to tread in something."

The other woman smells of old cheese and lemon-scented sunscreen.

"Thanks. Neither's he."

"Says you! His mother!"

"Stepmum. He's not my kid. I won't ever get over my shock when ... "

"What did he ... ?"

"When he was nine, the dog had a litter of seven puppies – nothing we couldn't sell. The pups were barely a fortnight old; he somehow found his daddy's shotgun and killed all of them except for one. Shot the mother too. Blood across the shed's inside wall. Near heart attack, I'm telling you."

"Horrible ... Lovely day."

"Too hot and moist for me. It didn't seem like a natural thing to do. Not for a child of nine. A useless act of killing ... "

"He was just bored. Little boys can be murdering bastards. My Timmy loved to help his daddy with the chickens."

"Yeah, Geoff said much the same thing when he found out. Oh look, they're going to drop the blackberries!"

We all watch as the bowl rises up in a parabolic curve, it stays upright, it reaches its peak and it seems, incredibly, as if no berries would be lost. No, the bowl has turned itself upside down, covered the world with blackberries and plopped rim first into the mud. Something emerges from the creek, a fiend to be barked at; woof! Unnatural creature, it has the shape of a man but skin of mud and algae and a couple of blackberries where its head might be.

The two women are laughing.

"He hehe heheheh hargh!"

Woof woof woof woof woof woof woof woof woof woof woof woof woof woof woof woof woof woof.

"Bitch! I asked you for help!"

Woof woof woof woof woof woof woof woof woof woof woof woof woof WOOF woof woof woof woof WOOF!

"Hehehheh har har hah!"

"Was going to, but had to put the berries down first, or we wouldn't have anything to bring back to your mother."

"Hehe hee! Don't worry about me, Anne dear."

Woof woof woof woof WOOF woof woof woof woof woof woof WOOF woof woof woof woof woof woof WOOF!

"Shuddup you barking, stray! You just don't want to get your clothes dirty and now I've got leeches in my trousers. Idiot girl."

"This is getting – erm, angry? I think we'll head back to the house?"

"Smooth move." The two women walk away.

Woof woof woof woof WOOF woof woof woof woof woof woof.

"Don't care about clothes," says the girl, and to prove it she steps, without hesitation, into the same mucky area that he'd fallen into. Filthy water comes up to her waist, she stands calmly beside him. "Don't know what you're complaining about. Lovely once you're in."

They clamber out; she picks a blackberry out of his hair and eats it, tearing her fingers on the thorns and her palms, sticky with blood and blackberry juice. Give us your hands little lady, let me lick your hands, I won't hurt you, I'm just a cute little puppy dog that hasn't tasted blood for so long.

"Get OFF you stinking mutt!"

Dirt drips from the edges of his t-shirt, cocoons itself into the creases of his jeans, clings to his hair in fresh drops like black pears. It slowly bakes in the late afternoon sun, drying into stringy clay before they go back to the house with their wretched bowl of blackberries, leaving nothing behind for a dog.

They call him Tom, the dog in the farm by the dairy, but he doesn't answer to the name. Black hair, muscles like rotating blades, slaughterhouse windows instead of eyes. He growls up towards me, claws sparking the earth. They love him at the dairy farm. Feed him pork sausages and tuna and if he sits still for half a second he gets bacon from their plates. I'd sit still as that dead tree trunk, but they don't give me nothing.

"Ya mangy mutt. Watch out ya don't give Tom worms, you rabies-infested sorry excuse for an animal."

Tom ignores me all day, but when night comes, a thing with his body visits me. And at night, the moon! Or more properly, the mooooooooooooooooooon!

I must eat and Tom-dog's stomach's never full. So we hurtle over fractured wire, up bent and lonesome roads, to where a group of sheep are waiting in a soft, patient cloud. It's here, the snowy wool, the mad shriek which flies from flesh as much as throats, the blood that spirits from white bodies like warm red light, rushing from a rising sun, scarlet over your shoulders, your nose, your eyes, dawn breaking at midnight. The other dog leaping from sheep to sheep like a monstrous, black, blazing, red-eyed frog, bouncing across bleeding lily pads.

And above there's still the moon, and still the moon, so round, so fierce, so glowing, the lord-dog of the ivory sphere. What are you doing rolling around my weak mind? Why work such madness on a poor hound's brain? Why grind and glisten and whistle white? You're here, you're there, so soft, so sweet, the muscles of an infant, the tingle of a spoon, lingering like a pale moth in this flowerless, dustless night.

Wazzat?

Someone comes suddenly up over a hill, his silhouette blackening the moon, the stars and glimmering gum trunks.

There's a click and a lowering of steel – I know I should have scarpered by now, but I can't look away from his shape. He seems to have wreathed the dark around his face and shoulders like dead vines. Only the curl of a night-blue lip and the unsteady reflections of what's in his hands can be seen. He smells of merciless, joyless, bloodless – "BANG!"

But I'm not hurt and I can sprint down the hill, down the road, into the scrub. Hawoooooooooo! And he who they called Tom is lying breathless at the farmer's boots.

Oh, moon! Whiter than the bones of my brother, long scattered over long grass. Creamier than maggots sprinkling my last meal. More perfect than the ever fresh scent of raw steak before flames. Moon! Give me strength!

I've broken into one of the murderer's storehouses, the door wasn't properly closed. I wipe my nose on the dirty shelves, make my marks in spots conspicuous, all the while smelling for something worth killing. Then, a presence unexpected. The living body of a woman. It shouldn't be here; it seems to know it doesn't belong. It has curled itself in the darkest, filthiest corner, wrapped itself in wool and is pretending to sleep. Massive rats skulk past the arrangement of human and bundles, squeaking to themselves in rancid voices about nasty secrets and poorly hidden sin.

Woof woof WOOF.

But there's a *cat* near the roof! Trotting amongst the sacks, its smug tail vertical, its eyes slit like rents in the earth.

WOOF WOOF WOOF!

A bare arm covers my nose.

"Shhhh."

I bark a little softer and let her stroke my chin, my back, with hands that smell of fire escape stairs and smoky tunnels, where people go searching for – I don't know what, I'm just a dog. I wonder if – what's that new smell drifting with the wind? Charred barbecues and gun powder and the creak of an opening door. That freezing silhouette again.

"You fu – Anne! What you doing here?"

"Didn't you tell me to come?" she says in a savage murmur like a breeze before a storm.

"That was ages ago Anne, you know it doesn't – You know I'm married with kids."

The cat prances about above my head, curling its claws, licking its arse, begging to be torn into shreds and scattered over farm, scrub and swamp.

She still grasps my fur, running her long fingers down my neck.

"I hope this dog isn't yours?"

"That mongrel? Kills my sheep. Broke in here like you."

"It's not very healthy. Hard to think of you as a married man."

"Is it?"

The cat vanishes.

"I've been gone for so long – time – can you lend me 50?"

"I – arc the police chasing?"

The light from his torch casts weird, flat shadows against the wool and her torn clothes. She is standing in the black and white like a nightmare in newsprint and he's trying to read her. "How did you escape?"

The smells are as obscure as the sweat of a being from another world, and I want to get out and chase the cat.

I push past the man, towards the door and towards the cat. Cats are everything that's wrong with the earth; if only people went to the trouble of exterminating them completely the air

would smell sweeter, mouths would be less hungry, it would rain in the right places, no one would die.

(He raises his gun).

Don't believe me?

Have you ever tried though? Eh? Eh? Aw, just shuddup and let a dog dream.

There have been too many clouds these past nights; I haven't been able to see the moon. I want to see it more than anything and don't know why. It's not as if the moon will make me happier, it'll just make me mad again. Ow howl! My leg! My ear! Why didn't I let him kill me?

Does anyone live here anymore? Land's sodden grey with floods, tumbled in cyclones and hung out to dry in the sun. Why do the birds return to this grim hole? Why do the filthy cats still live? Why does anything live? Can it be possible to feel so done and still breathe? Bloated flies shriek at my eyes. Blinking them away is so tiring I wonder how I used to manage it. And the magpies which I used to chase are all swooping and whooping about this pus-seeped head like it's a terrific joke.

Clack! Clack!

I can't even howl. I'm croaking like them. The humiliation!

Life's a thirsty moonless day, with the bitch locked high in her box. You've got dried mud in your ears and fleas nipping into the sags of your skin, fancying themselves more dog than you. And it might be hotter than your lungs or colder than your legs but you're burning into ashes and freezing solid all at once.

Wretched cats.

Treading through the rippling air, a woman. Perhaps I've smelt her before.

Clack clack! Pity me sweet lady! Are you lonely? Are you hungry? Are you death?

"You poor dog, eh? So this is what he did to you?"

Yes, bad things, mistress. I've suffered the way no creature has suffered. Now give us some meat, love! Yeah, yeah, pat me as much as you like, but some supper, woman!

She pats me near a bullet wound. My head wheels round and rips her hand.

Serves you right. Why couldn't you have left us alone? Pity's a nuisance when it doesn't come with a bone.

Dear One, I Turned Your Back Into a Tree

Nicole McNamara

I thought of drawing bats down your spine
I thought of how they'd fly from some
wasted willow tree towards the city lights.
I sketched it all out
(perfectly scratching it down).
I saw the bats fly from their sleeping places
on your ribs – they would circle your head
then move off in threes.
I had them hunt down strangers in the city.
They'd move as shadows should
if detached from our bodies.
The skin over your spine would grow cold
as city lights withdraw and Sunday
morning is born.
My bats, in their threes,
would return to their willow tree –
and I'd count them coming home.

My Soviet Mind

Madeleine Watts

Cities at night tremble like your teeth in the depths of winter. Like fingers on the buttons of the shirts of your lovers. It is hard to keep your footing in this city, easy to lose your way.

This morning he got on my bus. Four million people swarming around this city and he gets on my bus. It's almost a year to the day that I left. Now I try to forget. After all, we left it in shambles. Beat each other down through silence. And now we lie at loose ends, dispersed, avoiding the sight of it all.

But I think I've been imprinted. I think I'm like Pavlov's dog.

After all this time nothing has changed. He stopped, tried to wave at me. But I pretended I couldn't see or hear, lost in loud music and the window. He walked away, carried with the stream of morning people, and hanging on to the yellow rail he stared at my dark hair and my back. I could see him in the security monitor. I panicked and I tried to think how I could escape without having to do anything, refuse to be sensible or adult and run away. But I had to smile and pretend to be pleased. You're not supposed to speak, not on the bus, in places like this.

I have a Soviet mind, like a spy who has crossed the iron curtain. I lost all notions of a collective long ago, now I only want to stop losing control. It's why I chain-smoke and hide behind glasses. So he waved and smiled and I disappeared. I made him watch me walk away.

Night in the place where the city meets the sea. The imposing headlands and the concrete, a red light shining for every single person who drifts here, waiting for the ocean to rise up and carry them back to a real country. Because no one can say this is really home. We all hang in transit. This is the country we were exiled to. This is the place we come to go quietly mad.

In Hyde Park there are people screaming. Around the War Memorial people in glitter and black all swarm together in a heavy mass. A girl wearing nothing but an orange faux-fur coat twirls in circles holding a bottle of cheap white wine high over the heads of people trying to snatch it from her hands. A boy and a girl and another boy are kissing each other on a wooden bench usually slept on by one of those murmuring men you cross the street to avoid. Two men walk past, naked but for the leather straps that hold together their middle aged stomachs and leave everything open to the night. They mince along to the catcalls, one holding a shiny chain and pulling the other along by his thick neck. They are happy.

There are mounted police trying to keep the people from climbing the trees. When I was small I wanted to live in a tree. In the afternoons I would swing my legs and talk to myself until it got dark, sitting alone in the tree in my grandparents' front garden. It was like flying, being supported high up above the earth by strong arms, where no one could touch me, where I could sing myself to sleep and dream of everything good to come because everything was in the future.

Now I'm down on the ground, with some Russian boys, a bottle and my best friend. One of the boys is trying to hide the bad wine under his jacket in his lap so the police will pass us by. His face blurs into the background as he begins laughing and stroking my arm. He talks about girls and skin and the fight he had out in the suburbs last night, trying to touch the tips of my fingers I've kept fixed to the earth, but I feel nothing, breathe smoke into the air and pass the cigarette to the boy whose lap my friend sprawls in.

We were
the generation
who were taught,
"Just say no." No to
the strange men offering
sweets and comfort. No to
the alcohol, the drugs, the sex.
Because everything will kill you in
the end. We grew up on money and
AIDS and pixels and messy faces lying
in bed with people who weren't our parents
when they thought we were sleeping.

Just say no.

The police on horses come closer, ever closer. The blank-faced boy trying to hold my hand still talks into space located somewhere close to my ears. And the boy with my friend has talked me into a corner. I'm sitting with his jacket draped over my legs, so short is my dress that when I sit I have little to hide, especially when I'm sitting in the grass, trying to maintain something of myself. He is asking me about the future and talking about morality and Nietzsche. And the words come out of my mouth like charcoal. It never occurred to me that it was none of his business. His face manifests itself into the high court judge of my head, his fingers pointing and his mouth accusatory and loud.

In my head I rise up to a tenth-floor room above the harbour and hear the sirens shaking the people and their hearts from the trees. There is another world than this; another hemisphere, another mind. There must be. How else do we keep from going mad, so far away, in a place like this?

There is another boy, another Russian, pale and blond, hair falling into his mournful eyes. He speaks with a husk because he's caught between here and a cold place. And he's standing above me, wearing a suit, of all things, on a night like this, refusing to sit down and staring off into the distance where only police and hooligans roam. I want to pull on his hand and bring him down to face me. His eyes are deep and blue like the boy I used to love.

Gradually the park is cleared. Aggressive and tired the people on horses throw us all out. They have homes to get to and we are what remind them of their wasted youths. My friend and I hold hands and spin in unison. We talk our own language, clinging to each other for conviction. So we twirl and shout and when we separate I try to pet and hug the dark horses bought by the city to protect people from people like us, or so it would seem. It's the Eskimo blood in my veins and the general cement and decay.

We start walking away. People stream past without touching a hair on my pretty, precocious head. The Russians leave us on George Street and go inside a bottle shop, leaving us standing flooded by red-lit fluttering people. I lean against a street pole, electric light washing my face gold and strange. Three men in a taxi pull up beside us. They want to take us away. Arms appear around my neck and a gruff voice yells. They disappear and I'm standing under electric light with Russian arms holding me close.

Then the chemicals in my head begin to take hold.

I take a swig of the bad red wine offered to me from the hand of someone I've known only a few hours. We start walking again, against the people heading home. I oscillate wildly.

The city is young like us. Modern lights and varying shades of grey.

We walk and walk, losing people as we go along, as they peel off and merge into the shadows. I swallow and breathe fire into the southern skies and realise it's only me and the strange pale Russian boy in the suit, walking through streets I can't remember ever seeing before. The laneways fall silent; I begin to see things in negative. Through the walls and the concrete the sea ripples, reflecting red light, white light, and the stars I cannot see. Up there alone, upon the summit of night, a thread of intent leads us down to the water.

That map of the city you hold in your pocket is the map of my mind. The streets and the laneways are a book written long ago which map my memories. If you look long enough you will find bits of me written in the bricks and the gutters.

We have wandered into one of the new apartment complexes where entry is strictly forbidden, a security gate and a fat man sitting dozing at the entrance to keep the poor and the manic from stealing the boats of the wealthy and sitting on their wharf. He holds my hand tight and silently we run past the guard and the cameras and into the dark hiding places of the houses of the rich.

The wharf juts out into an enclosed harbour. To the left the looming bridge, firefly lights flitting across high over my head, making my pale skin a film screen, bathed in electric light. The buildings threaten above my head and shimmer. I have always thought this city was too hard to feel in, too hard to think in. We are locked inside between shadows and thoughts of space, revising the indexes of our lovers and friends and inconstant memories. Together we run across the wooden planks, collapsing on the edge, our legs dangling absently over the lunar sea.

It is cold, and the boy I barely know breathes Russian mist into the air. His voice still lingers in that far away hinterland, a solemn somnolence under icy eyes hidden behind pale hair. All night he has been trying to find a girl who refused to return his calls. Wounds unstitched stir in him unquiet ghosts which float around us as we sit together, his hand still holding mine.

He takes off his jacket and places it over my shoulders. "You are cold," he says in a gravely melancholy tone.

I'm nothing, but it stays where it is, warm from his body, big and awkward balancing on my shoulders. Exhaling and obscuring the watery stars he brings my arm to his chest. With his fingers, softly, he begins brushing lightly up and down, from my wrist to the crook of my elbow, tracing intricate patterns from his head into my white skin.

Tickles, he tells me. Tickles are what he does with girls. More intimate than anything else he knows, because it forces their eyes to meet. Up and down, a lullaby through my blood, to my whole body, and a shiver runs through me.

This, he tells me, is what nobody will do for him. He dreams of a train, an old Soviet tragedy from his childhood, and somebody is dying, but he cannot move. He can't remember where he came from. Every time he awakens from it he can feel ghostly fingers caressing his arm: tickles, like he does to me now.

Lights flicker over the city. His fingers flutter across my arm, and a breeze from across the world whistles around my legs hanging over the black water. His voice, his hands, whisper Russian spells into the night, battling through many negatives to what I am. By tides and faults of weather and the rain from Arctic places we come around.

I woke up on a bench on the edge of the sea, a light to my chest, my head on his knee.

The Passing Hour

Veronica Wagner

We are blackbirds warbling under liberty's compass of pleasures,
Wobbling free, wet-legged, and flocking out of the reeds as the storks do,
Slapping fishtail wings, then scouring skyward for glittering treasures –
We're uncertain creatures, half in seizures, and sing when we want to.

All the passion of the passing hour, no matter how winds blow,
Cannot move you, though the stars catch fire and oceans before you
Rumble hymns – your gaze is fixed and calmly you watch from a window,
Turn your countenance of ether-white away, let it ignore you.

Our slight hearts can't bear the kindling air, we are buffeted wildly;
Citrus-rich, the sunset sky alights and bedecks the wide water.
Sometimes in the hum and heat of spring, at your door you may find me,
Glaring madly in, unwilling to think of a cause for such torture.

Herons wade in silent pools beyond that blue cloudbank – there, dragons,
Copper-eyed, cavort in purple stone, bubbled up from volcanoes –
Serpents ring the world in shadowed fathoms, while birds in their billions
Storm the skies all summer, and yet you never discern what the heart knows.

Humula

Cassandra Taylor

We came here with our city haircuts, our city hearts; but we were eager and we were young. I almost hated the country, maybe for about half an hour – its vacant embrace, its eerie silent nights.

My friends and I, we are artists, we are artists making our escape. What we are running from I cannot tell, for it is a mystery even to me. But after six hours of driving through rolling hills you feel like you are leaving something behind. The buzzing hive of our metropolis? Our families, our jobs, our universities? Eddie Vedder urging us, loud, in the speakers.

Society, you're a crazy breed …

Urging us on, through this greenery to a home – what is to be our home for three nights.

We arrive in darkness, promising each other not to look at the sky until we arrive at our home. Our home at Humula. We spill from the van, necks craning to take it all in. Gasps. Silent releases of –

Oh, the stars …

Breath painting against the sky. Attempts to describe the night sky in deep country will always be feeble; even Van Gogh didn't capture the extent of our starry starry night. Millions and millions of tiny gems, sparkling, sprayed against pure ebony, shooting, glistening. A fitting frame for such vast emptiness.

Gently comes the morning and the birds begin to orchestrate the soundtrack for winter. I feel that the sun would like to join in too, but the music of the sun is visual: and so it spreads, golden, waking the flowers' timid bloom and drying the frosty ground. Adventure is the order of the day. We are met with views of hills as far as one can see, dappled sunlight mingling below deciduous trees. I chase some rams before thinking better of it; what if they gore me with their horns?

Death is here, declarative in the chaos of perfect order. It is not feared, nor is it destruction, although at first it is obscene. I catch myself thinking

Shouldn't someone clean that up?

as though it were unnatural to die. No. No one will sweep it out of my line of vision; it shall rot openly in the field, ribs protruding from a heap of wool, maggoty mouth wide-open, legs a few metres away.

I feel in my heart that everything is as it should be here. There are no bruised lemons, no abused dogs and no wasted hearts. And the people – *oh the people!* They love you immediately, they welcome you into their homes, they give you fresh eggs. They tell you about their lives without being prompted, beam with pride about their crops and vineyards and ducks and horses. They ask about your life, checking that you aren't wasting any opportunities.

They have vision.

They build us a bonfire with 14 trees: it is the size of a small house. We stand away from it, our faces burning. We use entire branches to roast marshmallows. Children run around the fire, they spell their names out with sparklers.

We drink wine and watch the community come to life.

The elements are raw here: fire is glorious and cold air makes frost and earth covers your boots and the water is clean.

The locals gather and glance at us with mild curiosity. Immediately I am defensive – *stop judging me!* – before I realise my own insecurity. We are neither envied nor pitied – we are simply city. We crouch in our coats, our tight jeans. They stand in their flannels and watch. Nothing here connotes or denotes. Things simply are. I wonder if pretension is even in these people's vocabularies. We are invited to church. We eagerly accept. We double the congregation. They have no music, so they sing *a cappella*, from hymnbooks. We are encouraged. They are encouraged. We are all in love.

Ben sketches me one lazy afternoon. The girls do watercolors and Nik fiddles on the guitar. We sit until we are sunburnt but we are satisfied. Later we will huddle around the fireplace and I will probably fall asleep. Maybe I will dream of *Blue Poles*, maybe I will wonder why it made me cry again. Maybe I'd rather not know.

When we leave, we leave sadly. We've grown fond of this house, our house, even if there was a dead bat under our bed, copper-coloured water in the kitchen and stray sheep with cancerous growths. It all adds to the charm, we think. We want to steal the *Bob Dylan's Greatest Hits* record and *The Complete Works of Oscar Wilde* book but we don't. Now we leave this behind, piling into the van with our crocheted blankets and pillows. We smile and drive away, knowing we will be back.

Walter and Millie

Tinny Hon

Walter picked up the bunch of yellow daisies wrapped in cellophane and ribbon from the passenger seat. He grabbed the bag from the floor. The Perrier-Jouet bottle clanked against the Jameson bottle. The house was dark but for the glow of the TV.

"Sweetheart, I'm home."

His wife was sitting on the lounge watching her favourite soap opera. "Oh, sweetheart, happy anniversary." He leant over and kissed her cheek. She didn't look up. "I have a very special dinner planned for us tonight. Why don't you get dolled up, Millie, I've bought champagne, we'll make an evening of it."

At the table, Walter poured champagne into her glass. It was her favourite. He waited for the bubbles to subside before topping it up. He pushed a strand of hair out of her face, cupped her chin and tilted her head back so that their eyes could meet.

"Darling, you are as beautiful as the day we met." There was a faint smile on her face but nothing in her eyes. He served her half a lobster, squeezing lemon over it for her. He ladled a little melted butter over hers and then his own. He broke the bread and put a piece on her side plate before dipping his own piece into the garlicky butter and taking a bite.

"I do love that dress, Millie. It matches your eyes, I've always loved your blue eyes, so bright and happy but still serious. But they're always so serious now."

When he'd finished with his dinner, he frowned a little to see Millie's untouched plate. "Darling, you'll waste away."

He knew she wasn't going to eat it so he took it away and brought out Millie's favourite chocolate cake.

"Dessert, darling? You'll eat dessert won't you?" He served her anyway and ate his in silence. The phone rang but he ignored it. He never answered the phone during dinner.

After dinner, when all the dishes had been done and Millie's favourite quiz show was finished, Walter opened the whiskey. He had a drink, then another, then one more. He showered and got ready for bed. Millie was already in bed in her filmy nightdress. Walter lay beside her. He didn't know if he should just read or if he could … possibly, maybe … he couldn't. It had been so long, he couldn't anymore. Millie didn't mind anymore. She wouldn't care if they didn't make love on their anniversary.

In the morning, Walter ate his toast and drank his tea. Millie hadn't stirred so he made her a cup of tea and put it on a tray with today's paper and one of last night's daisies in a little vase. He put the tray on her bedside table, then dressed for work and kissed her goodbye.

At the office he couldn't concentrate. He shuffled a few papers around his desk. The messages light flashed on his telephone but he didn't want to talk to anyone. He ignored it. At lunchtime, he told his boss he didn't feel well.

Boss said, "Yeah, Walter, you look like shit," and sent him home for the day.

Walter went to the bar downstairs. He had a double Jameson and went home.

At home, the house was quiet. It was lunchtime but Millie was still in bed. The tea beside her was cold, the paper still folded. Walter took the tray to the kitchen. He came back and gently shook Millie by the shoulder.

"Sweetheart, it's me. Do you want to get up for a while? I've come home early. Come on, we can have lunch together."

While Millie watched TV, Walter made them a sandwich each. He had Millie's leftover lobster flesh in his. He added a big dollop of the delicious homemade mayonnaise Millie had made the other day; she always added a touch of mustard and squeeze of lemon to it. She had Vegemite. He didn't bother buttering hers but then felt bad for not bothering and threw it in the bin. He made her a fresh one with butter. He knew she wouldn't have complained but ... she used to be the gourmet and gourmand, the one with the complex palate that could always taste the things Walter's was too undiscerning to discern, the one whose day revolved around what to cook next; now she was having Vegemite sandwiches for lunch. He tucked last night's whiskey bottle under his arm, took their plates to the living room and sat down next to Millie.

"Here, sweetheart."

He put her sandwich plate on her lap. "You know, I was thinking we could ... "

The phone interrupted. Walter went to the phone and saw his daughter's number in the display.

"Millie, d'you want to talk to Judy? No, no, didn't think so. Me neither." He let it go to the machine. Walter took a drink from the bottle. He ate his sandwich quickly and drank more, almost all the whole bottle, before he started crying.

"Millie. I just don't know. What's going to happen to us?"

121

He cried for an hour. Millie just watched TV.

"Millie, please, say something. Please … "

Walter went out the back door and tossed the empty whiskey bottle into the recycling bin. He went further out into the yard and brought in the laundry. He tipped the laundry out onto the kitchen table and folded their clothes and all the sheets. He went into the bedroom and put their clothes away and changed the sheets on the bed.

That night they went to bed in silence. Walter looked at Millie, eyes closed and face peaceful. He lay down next to her and sobbed quietly. Under the sheets, he reached for his wife's hand and held it til he fell asleep.

Walter woke feeling inexplicably happy. He looked over at Millie and smiled at his wife of 25 years. She was still so pretty in the morning light, just like when they'd first met. Millie had been the receptionist at his first office job. After three months of polite "Good mornings" and "Good evening, Miss Stevensons", Walter mustered up the courage to ask if she would dine with him.

When Millie said yes he was so happy he hummed and almost danced his way home. That Saturday evening, he picked her up from her parents' house and took her to the nicest French restaurant he could afford, even though he was worried about ordering in French and having to choose wine. Turned out he needn't have worried – Millie was quite the wine expert and he watched her shine when the sommelier came to their table. She looked beautiful that night, in a cornflower blue dress, her regal neck layered in blue beads. Her hair was swept back and up, pinned with a jewelled clip, different to how she always had it pulled back in a low ponytail at the office. That night, they talked and laughed and dined on grilled lobsters with melted garlic butter. Walter hadn't known it was Beaujolais time and he would never have ordered a red to go with shellfish but Millie knew. They finished with a shared dessert of meringues topped with intricate peaks of Chantilly cream, and brandies. It was the first of 12 grand dinners before he asked her to marry him at that same restaurant. He couldn't help jumping out of his seat a little when she'd said yes.

Now, he couldn't take Millie to fancy restaurants anymore. But he didn't care. He was just happy that they were still together. He decided not to think about how much longer they might have together, not today. As usual, he laid out some clothes for her before going to shower and dressing himself. When breakfast was ready, he helped Millie to the table. Today he made eggs Benedict, making hollandaise from scratch like Millie had shown him. He even thought Millie looked happy. Was she smiling?

"Oh! Sweetheart, I've just had a wonderful idea. Let's go for a drive today!" It hadn't occurred to Walter before, but he could quite easily take Millie out in the car. Maybe somewhere with a pretty view on the seaside. He ate his breakfast quickly and helped himself to some of Millie's before tidying up the kitchen. Walter got his road map from the bookcase. He found his and Millie's sunglasses and made a thermos of tea.

He helped Millie into the car and buckled her in. He ran back inside to get the thermos and was just pulling the door shut behind him when he heard the phone ring. No, he thought. He shut the door and joined Millie in the car. "Ready?" Her eyes said yes.

The radio was starting to cut out as they rolled down the freeway, out of Sydney. Walter turned it off but continued singing.

"Wasn't this a good idea? Wasn't it? You haven't been out all week. You must be bored, stuck at home all day. It's such a nice day!" Walter drove them to a small seaside town and followed the signs to the scenic lookout. From the car park, high over the sea, he could see the town below, the shoreline white on blue as it rolled back and forth over the golden arc of sand, all those broccoli like treetops crowding around the neat rows of houses.

"Isn't it pretty up here Millie?" He smiled at her. "I'll go get us something to eat, okay? I'll be right back."

From the queue at the kiosk, Walter looked back at Millie in the car. She was leaning against her window, gazing out to sea. Walter wondered if people thought she looked funny but no one seemed to pay any attention to her as they walked past, snapping photos of each other with the view behind them. Walter thought she looked lovely but maybe her hair needed doing. It was all messed up where it was pressed against the glass. He'd never done her hair for her before, and this week he'd only been brushing it, but maybe he would have to learn one or two of her favourite hairstyles. He bought two sandwiches and two packets of chips. In the car, he poured himself a cup of tea into the thermos' lid-cup and after having a drink, he poured one for Millie and put it on the dash in front of her.

It was dusk as they pulled into their street. He stopped the car in their driveway and looked around, checking no neighbours were out, watering gardens or whatever, before opening the front door and returning to the car to get Millie out. He turned on the TV for Millie because one of her shows was about to start. He went out to lock the car when he saw Judith walking up the path.

"Dad! Dad! Where have you been?"

"Oh! Judy! Umm … nowhere." He was stricken to see her.

"Dad, I've been calling and calling. You weren't at work yesterday and I can never get you at home. I've been leaving messages, why haven't you called me back, Dad?"

"I ... "

"Where's mum? The hospital said she didn't go in this week."

"She's ... "

Judith ran inside and stopped in the living room doorway. There was her mother, sitting on the lounge, in front of the TV. Her cannula, not connected to her drip, peeked out from the neckline of the blue dress her father had always liked. Her mother was wearing the white shoes she hated, the ones that were too tight. Her lipstick was smeared and crookedly put on. Her hair was matted and untidy. When Walter heard Judith scream, he raced inside.

"Dad! What's going on? When did Mum die?"

A Self-Reflexive Cycle

Paul Ellis

I don't know what I'm going to do in the future. I sometimes say with much conviction what it is I will do with my life as if doing so could hide the fact that I don't have a clue.

If I was truly any different to my parents then I'd move out of home and stop taking their money.

I think I'm different to everyone. I'm convinced that I'm special. That I'll 'make it'. I don't know what I'll make it in but I'll make it. I think I'm smart too. I think I have this crazy type of intelligence that doesn't express itself in essays or exams but is very powerful and very real. I'm really very fragile even though I pretend to have everything worked out.

I recognise the exact moments in my life where I have the chance to make myself a happier person but I never do anything about it.

I refuse to do anything hard. I'd be a better student if I liked what I was doing. As long as I don't apply myself I can never fail.

I really want to meet a nice girl. I should work on developing some personality. I want to be interested in things. People that are interested in things are interesting. Except 'zany' people. Zany people pretend to have many interests but really just have one interest: to seem interesting. They are as a result the least interesting type of person. Uni is full of them. I'm aware this little anecdote breaks the 'confessional' style of this memoir/short-story/creative non-fiction/I-truly-don't-know-will-leave-it-up-to-you-oh-kind-and-beautiful-*ARNA*-editor but I'm at such a stretch for content that I'm including it anyway.

I wish I could write a story with characters and narrative and subtlety. I wish this was poetic. Maybe I could write a real story but I'm too lazy to try. That's a theme of this story in case you hadn't picked up on it. Maybe this story will stand out if it's overly self-referential. But everything is postmodern these days. This isn't original. Was claiming my own unoriginality original? I'm sure it's been done. ENDLESS SELF-REFLEXIVE CYCLE. Kill me.

I avoid accepting responsibility for my failures by telling myself I just haven't found my passion. I'm passionate about finding my passion. I'm passionate about being passionate about finding my passion. I might as well tell you I'm ripping this idea off Dave Eggers. The whole self-reflection/inner dialogue thing – all Dave Eggers. Read *A Heartbreaking Work of Staggering Genius*. I'll make a footnote of it for you. Arts reference! How appropriate for an Arts students' journal!

Publish me! I want to see my name in print!

Our Souls Are Our Shadows

Nicole McNamara

You take my arm to fight the shadows back.
Armed with a sewing needle and thread
{I get ready}.
And we'd chase the pigeons along the pavement,
prepared to fight them if necessary.

What harm can two kids
{afraid of the dark and of the shadows that we make}
do with coloured cotton on a Sunday afternoon?

Afraid of the dark and of the shadows that we make
breaking away – I try to sew the pigeons to the ground,
to connect them to themselves
{to their souls}.

I'll build monuments to those birds that chose not
to stay with their souls –
they are braver than me.

Afterword

All writers have big egos.

Speaking as an aspiring writer, I know this to be true (and George Orwell would agree). That is why it has been such a humbling experience to work on *ARNA*, as students all across campus sent their collections of carefully arranged words, waiting for a reader.

When we started on *ARNA* all those months ago, it was with the firm conviction that students deserve to be heard. Too often dismissed as idealistic, naïve or even ignorant, we felt that students deserve a place to articulate their opinions, to muse in prose, to rhyme a couplet or two. We may not have the big stage yet, but journals like *ARNA* help nurture the artful sentence constructions of tomorrow.

I am grateful for this small glimpse into the pensive, quirky and witty minds of my peers and endlessly inspired by the enthusiasm and creativity of this year's editorial and launch team. Working on *ARNA* has been an amazingly fulfilling experience.

Thank you to SASS President Khym Scott for your guidance and powerhouse design skills. Thanks to the Treasurer, Marina Lauer, for watching our purse-strings and keeping us on the ball: Oh, to be adept with numbers! To Callie, my co-editor, who developed the knack to quell my rising hysteria at any given point in time: this ride wouldn't have been as fun without you.

And last, but not least: thank you to every last writer – published or not – for sharing your words, and for trusting us with your egos.

Nancy Lee

Thanks To

University of Sydney Faculty of Arts

University of Sydney Union

Clubs & Societies Office

Sydney Arts Students Society

Sydney University Press

Scott Brownless

Lachlan Carey

Thomas William Clement

Julian Larnach

Luke Martin

Jordan McClellan

Rachel Molden

Agata Mrva-Montoya

Jacqueline Munro

Jennifer Ngai

Phillip Roser

Tom Walker

www.ingramcontent.com/pod-product-compliance
Lightning Source LLC
Chambersburg PA
CBHW051514260626
47162CB00008B/2958